OUR NEW
NORMAL

A JOURNAL OF TRAGEDY,
HOPE, AND INSPIRATION

CYNDI KAMPS

GO BOB
PUBLISHING

Cover, interior book design, and eBook design
by Blue Harvest Creative
www.blueharvestcreative.com

OUR NEW NORMAL

Published by
GO BOB Publishing

ISBN-13: 978-0692396315
ISBN-10: 0692396314

INTRODUCTION

Bob Kamps was 50 years old when he suffered a severe closed head injury at the hands of an incompetent driver. As a crew member for the Michigan Department of Transportation (MDOT), he routinely shoveled tar into the many pot holes on Michigan's weather beaten roads. It was a Tuesday evening at 6:30pm when the driver of an SUV slammed into two of the MDOT crew members resulting in Bob's life changing horrific injury (the second crew member sustained minor injuries) During the first year of Bob's fight back to life, his wife Cyndi kept a journal. The journal helped to keep family, friends, and coworkers informed of Bob's journey and documented the many good, bad and horrific events Bob faced on his fight back. This book contains those journal entries — unedited and left just as they were entered during those tragic, triumphant and tumultuous days.

ABOUT BOB KAMPS

Husband, dad, grandpa, brother, son, uncle, neighbor, friend, golf partner, corn hole player and so much more. Quiet, strong, rooted in faith and my rock not to mention my better half.

On Tuesday, February 8, 2011, our normal world was turned upside down when Bob was hit by a car. He sustained a critical and severe closed head injury and so our new "normal" begins.

OUR NEW
NORMAL

FEBRUARY 2011

FEBRUARY 11—8:06 AM

Tuesday, February 8, around 6:30 pm, Bob sustained a direct hit by a car traveling +45 mph. He sustained a critical and severe head injury and now begins the journey to recovery. Here's what you need to know:

> ICP = intracranial pressure - this needs to be below 20 - you and I have a brain pressure of 0 to 2. This can go up to around 5 if you stand on your head. Bob's ICP was up as high as the low 30's.

Brain Activity or what I call his brain calmness - this needs to be around 40. The point of this is to keep his brain calm so he can heal. Basically like keeping a broken bone in a cast and immobile until it heals. Bob's brain activity was around 80.

Bob is in a medically induced coma to keep his brain calm and to maintain high oxygen levels. These things will help minimize the already traumatic brain injury he received. His ICP was fluctuating in the high 'teens and would jump to high 20's to 30's whenever he had any activity - even the slightest bit of movement made his ICP go up. This morning around 6:30, Bob's ICP was around 5...THIS IS A HUGE YAY! It even went down to 0 while I was chatting with him this morning. Today and tomorrow are still critical days for Bob. Brain swelling occurs within the first 3 to 5 days after a trauma so we're not out of the woods for that yet. Hoping by Sunday we can start with a "what's next" plan. Because this is a brain injury, nobody knows what will happen. It's a slllllooooowwwwwww process with no expectations and nothing to benchmark. Everybody's recovery is different. It's hour by hour right now. The good news - Bob's ICP and brain activity right now are fantastic. He's over achieving when it comes to oxygenation, which is a great thing. He's being a model patient and doing what he needs to do to heal. Both of us thank God for our incredible network of friends and family. You all deserve a huge THANK YOU for being so supportive and keeping us in your thoughts and prayers. Every prayer is obviously helping. Thank you, thank you, thank you. More to come as I learn more about his journey through this mess.

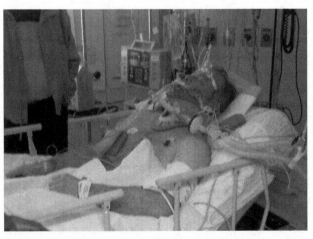

FRIDAY, FEBRUARY 11

OK, so Bob and I talked about doing something new in 2011. This is not what I had in mind but so it goes. I've learned waaayyyy more new stuff in the past 48 hours than I ever wanted to learn about closed head injuries.

Classic Bob!!!

Periodically they have to check his reaction for pain. Every time they do that he gets the hiccups! I think it's his way of protesting the pain stimulation. Made me laugh.

FRIDAY NIGHT

Days 3, 4 and 5 are the most critical and we've gotten thru day 3 with some concerns. ICP and brain calmness were all over the place. The farther away we get from the time of the accident, the less chance there is for critical things to happen. Sunday can't get here fast enough! It's going to be a long weekend.

As for me, yes, I'm sleeping and eating. Thanks to great friends who brought me lots of wonderful gluten free snacks. I'll be the wife that gains weight during this ordeal! :) I listened to everyone's advice and decided to sleep as much as I can tonight to get ready for whatever comes next. Good night and keep praying!

SATURDAY, FEBRUARY 12

Even though it's hard for anyone to tell me what to expect today, the nurse did say that he expects to have some issues with Bob's cranial pressure. It's common on day 4 to have the ICP fluctuate. Right now, Bob is responding to medication to keep the ICP low so that's a good thing. It's manageable and hopefully will stay that way. We're going to leave him alone today and allow him to continue to heal. Today and tomorrow are going to be a crazy ride so thank you for the continued prayers and support.

SATURDAY AFTERNOON

Bob's making them work for their money today. His brain is seizing, which means the numbers are spiking and dropping all over the place. They increased his sedation and now the numbers look good again. He is getting an EEG right now but the strobing light and popping noise they use was giving me a headache so I had to leave. Hopefully we know the results of the EEG soon. I don't know if this whole thing is a good thing or bad thing. I think it just is. It's just part of what Bob's course of recovery requires.

EEG Info — apparently there is no seizure activity, which is good. The brain is just being active and then quieting down. More sedation for tonight. The drug used to reduce swelling is being given more and more often with reduced effects, which is not good. We're in the danger zone now. It's going to be a long night. I'm going to sit with Bob so I'll post more tomorrow. Keep thinking positive and thanks for all of the support and prayers!

EARLY DAY 5

Bob has the doc stumped. His ICP will not come down but all his other numbers look fine. Doc had to get his textbooks out and do some research...ha! Leave it to Bob to give the docs a puzzle to solve. For now, more sedation and will reassess in the morning. Good night.

SUNDAY, FEBRUARY 13

Well, Bob's being Bob. Still puzzling. His ICP went way up to 56 while the doc and I were talking in his room. I don't think he likes us talking about him so we stepped out and his ICP went down to 19. Still don't know what to do. All his other numbers look great. Potential for an even deeper sedation, which will knock him completely out...no brain waves. That's a good thing because we still want his brain to rest and not have to do ANYTHING.

BTW — a lot of you have asked if Bob sustained any other injuries and the answer is a great big NO! Yay! It's all in his head :) At least all his energy can go to healing his brain and nothing else.

SUNDAY NIGHT, FEBRUARY 13

We are a whole lot more optimistic tonight then last night. The numbers, while still fluctuating, are staying within an acceptable range. They aren't real happy with the fluctuations but at this point, it is what it is. I told the nurse I was feeling more optimistic and he said that tonight was going to be a better night. Yay!

I was able to go home for about 5 hours today and do laundry and clean...very therapeutic to do something normal. I even took about a 30 minute nap while the last load was drying. I was pretty impressed with myself. However...note to self... check pockets for Kleenex before washing pants!!!!!

HAPPY VALENTINE'S DAY!

Bob is still givin' 'em a run for their money. ICPs are still a problem but his CT scan was good, EEG was good, oxygenation level IS good...he's still puzzling the doc. Talking about a different drug therapy to see if that will help. They still have plenty of tricks up their sleeves. Just need to figure out what Bob needs.

Thank you to everyone for everything! Turning on the furnace, snow blowing our driveway, shoveling our walk, magazines on my front seat, food, mail pick-up, parties in the "Man Room", picking up the truck, sending cards and well wishes, figuring out what the heck to do with the hot tub, covering my job responsibilities...all of this has been a source of strength for me. That's a whole lot of stuff I don't have to worry about right now and that's HUGE! Thank you all. I wish there was something more I could do to express my gratitude so please know that it is GREATLY appreciated.

Here we go again. Bob's getting another CT.

We're back in the woods. Another long day here. Crap! I'm going to need a really good anti-aging cream and hair coloring after this. I've aged 10 years in 5 days! Pray and think positive today!!!!

VALENTINE'S UPDATE

CT shows no change, which is good. Cranial pressure is still fluctuating but staying between 8 to 18. OK-ish. They really don't like it to fluctuate but at least it's within range. He's gone backwards today but not as far back as we were early Sunday morning. Let's hope we don't go back there again!

I knew I forgot something. Thank you to the entire MDOT Kzoo crew for the cafeteria food card. Awesome! I have to say I've eaten more grilled chicken in the last 6 days than I knew existed but at least it's giving me the energy I need to support Bob. I also thank all of you for giving me the means to stay at a local hotel so I'm only 10 minutes away rather than 45. You guys are truly a great crew!

Apparently I'm really Bob's valentine because I was sitting with him for less than 5 minutes and his pressure went up to 31. I stood up, put the chair away and started out of the room and his ICP dropped 10 points. Since we want the ICP to be as low as possible, I left. It's crazy how sensitive he is...did I actually just type that? "Sensitive"? I don't want the guys to think he was some kinda mamby pamby so let's just say his brain senses changes in stimulation. That doesn't mean Bob was necessarily in touch with his feminine side. Not that there's anything wrong with that. And as you can see by my ramblings, I've officially arrived in la la land. Perhaps I need some of those brain drugs :)

END OF DAY 6

Still can't figure this out. Same course of treatment tonight -sedation (dipravan) and diuretic (manitol) to decrease swelling. Getting to the top doses of these two meds AND giving them more frequently. Still talking about switching sedation meds and putting him out for next 72 hours-ish. Still don't know if that's bad or good. Basically, nothing much is different than on Sunday afternoon. Where is this all going? I have no idea. What will happen tomorrow? I have no idea. We were all so hoping that Sunday would mark the cross road of his recovery but he is just simply taking longer than expected. I feel like a broken record so maybe tomorrow I'll have good news and exciting progress to report.

BEGINNING OF DAY 7

I wish I could just "yadda, yadda, yadda" this away (Seinfeld 1990's). Update this morning - sedation and anti-inflammatories are still working. That's good news. Cranial pressure went down to 8 while I was rubbing his foot and then it went up to 23 while I was talking to the nurse so we shut up and I went back to rubbing his foot. That only worked for about 30 seconds and pressure started going up again. These numbers are better than yesterday so we're hoping and praying for a better day today. I'll leave him alone again today. I keep thinking about Aerosmith song, "Living on the Edge." I'm not sure this is what Steve Tyler was talking about but we've been on the edge for 6 full days now. Time for Bob to start moving away from the edge to solid ground again!

UPDATE FOR DAY 7

Trying new drug in addition to manitol. Still can't get the cranial pressure down and had to increase his sedation again. Trauma surgeon will be talking with us this afternoon, which I can't figure out. The trauma guy on Monday said Neuro is leading Bob's care but I haven't talked with a Neuro person since Sunday morning. What the *&^% are these doctors doing? I'm going to have to go off on one of them again. It's the only way I can get them to listen to me!!!! Plus it makes me feel better :)

SEMI-POSITIVE NEWS.

Doc started new drug to help with swelling. Basically, it's a high dose of salt and is supposed to dry up the fluid around the brain. First dose at around 2 and so far so good. ICP went right down within range. Sooooo, I'm hoping that this is a turn for the better. We'll know more tomorrow.

As for me, I had a little tantrum about not seeing any docs since yesterday morning and not seeing Neuro since late Saturday. All of a sudden, all the docs were here. Go figure! :)

TUESDAY NIGHT, FEBRUARY 15

It's been 7 days since the accident. Seems like one continuous long day. Right now, Bob's cranial pressure is going up and staying up again. For the past 3 days the nurses have been working tirelessly around the clock to control the pressure. Tonight will be more of the same. I had to leave because with every fluctuation my heart would break just a little bit more. Sure hope tomorrow brings us some good news!

One more thing — there is a group of 40 cloistered nuns that know about Bob's accident and they are now praying for him. They started this evening. It gives me a great sense of peace knowing that all of you are praying for him as well.

HAPPY HUMP DAY!

I gotta believe that today Bob will get over the hump!

He had an OK-ish night, which is better than the last 3 nights. He had a few hours where his pressure actually stayed down! There were a few courses of treatment given to bring it down and those drugs are still working. These are all good things. Today we expect more of the same with fewer intervals of increased pressure. At this point, I'll take any positive thing I can get!

Now is the time for lots of PRAYERS!!!! Bob is now getting Pentabarbitol. This is a deep sedation and even less stimulation is allowed. I won't be able to go into his room for at least the next 3 days but probably more like 5. If this doesn't work, we're running out of options. I can handle being away from him for 3 to 5 days but not forever so please keep praying and thinking positive! We've reached an even more dangerous zone now.

EVENING UPDATE DAY 8

I just spoke to the nurse and as of right now, the Pentobarb is working. I'm afraid to get my hopes up again so we'll just be thankful that right now, his cranial pressure is low (good) and his oxygenation is high (good). I decided to come home and get some clean clothes and possibly some sleep to prepare for whatever comes next. This is a crazy ride that no one should ever have to take but we're all thankful that Bob is getting outstanding care at the best trauma center in Michigan.

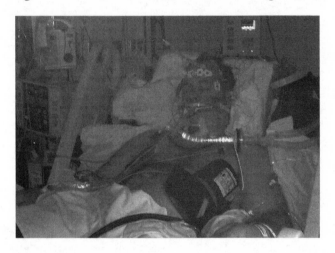

THURSDAY, FEBRUARY 17...RIGHT?

I can't remember what day it is anymore.

I hate to complain about a headache given Bob's situation but I have a doozie this morning. Hopefully the 2 Aleve I just took knock it out. I realize I'm not eating enough. It's not like I'm eating a Thanksgiving dinner everyday so maybe I should work on that. Another day of watching the numbers and praying for the best. I finally figured out that this is all a juggling act between what's good for his head and what's good for his body. The Pentabarb is controlling the ICP. However, he is still on the high doses of salt (they refer to it as the 3%) and that is messing with his sodium levels... naturally. They had to turn down the 3% and his ICP went up to the high teens. That's an acceptable level though. Today we'll watch his oxygenation too. There are some potential issues developing with his lungs because this is day 9 on a respirator. I've also noticed that he likes to throw us a curve ball in the late mornings and we're left trying to figure out what it all means...will the new drugs work, what will they do, what are we watching for (poor grammar, hope mom is reading this)? It's only 9 AM so for the sake of my headache, I pray he is stable today at the very least!

NO CURVE BALL YET...

It seems that the pentobarb continues to work. The doc is doing a thoricotamy (I have no idea how to spell that) to remove the fluid around Bob's right lung. This will help with his oxygenation levels. He's been having difficulty keeping on the gases...ha! If you only knew Bob as well as I do, you would know how funny that really sounds :) So, more balancing numbers and making sure his body can handle what they're giving him for his brain. I'm trying to stay in the moment and take the positive stuff today rather than waiting for something else to go wrong. All in all, this is a better day relatively speaking.

Ooops...Thoracotomy is when they remove something big. Bob is actually having a thorasentisis, which is removing just the fluid. Geez, I really didn't care to ever have to know that but I guess I'm glad I know the difference now.

...AND 10 MINUTES LATER...

Now we're only doing an ultra sound on his lung to see what's really there. Perhaps a thoracentesis tomorrow. I'm seriously going to beat some one up pretty soon! I guess the good news is ultra sounds aren't invasive and there's really no risk.

ANOTHER CURVE BALL...

ICP is hanging in the low 20s. Not good. This is going to be another very long day. Neuro doc should be here this morning to discuss what's next. My brain can't even fathom what's next so I'm just hanging on for the ride at this point. I will post more after I know more. CRAP!

AFTERNOON UPDATE, DAY 10

Well, so the roller coaster continues. We were going down hill this morning and now we're on our way back up. Good thing I don't have motion sickness!!! :)

Bob's ICP went down to 11 and is pretty much staying in the teens right now. The shadow on or in his lung really wasn't his lung. Apparently it was his diaphragm causing a shadow...yay! Nothing bad to report about the lung and his oxygen level is back above 30. And we'll just keep riding high on this little piece of good news for now.

My in-laws and my parents are sitting with me now so I'm outnumbered and have to eat and sleep and behave. I feel like I'm 2 again :) Seriously though they are a Godsend. I don't know what I'd do if I was sitting here all by myself day in and day out. I think I would be in the Kalamazoo mental hospital by now. Again, I am incredibly fortunate to have great family, friends, neighbors, and coworkers. Thank you all and keep thinking positive!

WOW...DAY 10, FRIDAY NIGHT, FEBRUARY 18

I can't believe it's been 10 days since the accident. Crazy how time seems to stand still when these things happen. More of the same tonight — managing numbers and keeping the faith. At least for today and into tonight, the ICP is within range and oxygen levels are up. Praying this continues to get better from here. I'm able to sleep at home, which allows me to get prepared for whatever comes next. Who knows what tomorrow will bring. Here's a funny one for ya - mom and dad came up from Florida and are staying with me. Dad turned the heat up to 75! Not sure our furnace has ever been above 68. It's now rather tropical in here.

SATURDAY, FEBRUARY 19, DAY 11

Doc wants to do a bronchoscopy this morning to take a peek at Bob's lungs to see if anything is going on. I spoke with the nurse early this morning and he said Bob was pretty stable all night. The nurse wasn't "chasing after him" to keep him stable...positive thing to hold on to today. ICP went up when they messed with him but went back down when they stopped. That's to be expected since he's been doing that since we got here.

Beautiful sunrise this morning. Been a long time since I was up early on a Saturday to enjoy that.

PS - I turned the heat down at home...ha!

SATURDAY EVENING, DAY 11

Holy crap again. Now it's the oxygen levels. Not good. Of course it was the trauma surgeon who told me and of course he phrased it in a way that was awful. We know Bob is hanging on the edge of disaster and has been for 11 days but why do the trauma guys need to keep saying everything with such a dramatic slant? Now I'm panicked again. In order to get the oxygen level up, the settings on the ventilator are going to be changed. We should see the effects of this in the next hour or two. Trauma surgeon words, "this is life critical." Well DUH! What an a$$. It's been life critical for 11 days! I'm staying here tonight but hope and pray that I'm not needed and that this adjustment in the ventilator works. Apparently we're getting to the end of our options on improving Bob's oxygenation. Another long night at the NCU. At least I have soft Kleenex now and not the free sand paper they put in these waiting rooms.

Holding on to the good stuff. The adjustments in the ventilator worked and the oxygen levels went up. At this moment (actually I should say as of 8:00 pm) the numbers have stabilized. His vent is on some funky rhythm that makes me want to hold my breath when I'm able to sit with him. It's like one big breath in, two little breaths forcing more air in and then one big breath out. Very weird but who cares. It's working. Nurse told me now was a good time to go because the numbers are good so I'm staying at the hotel tonight. The nurses are absolutely fantastic and I know they will call if anything changes...bad or good. I'm sure sleep will be out of my grasp but I can at least rest. I'm praying that tomorrow there isn't any more TRAUMA DRAMA!!!

SUNDAY, DAY 12

The highs are getting fewer and the lows and getting bigger. They were able to turn down the oxygen level on the ventilator to 80% last night but then Bob crashed. His oxygen level tanked and his pressure went up. The doc suctioned him again, which helped. As of 5AM, his numbers were stable again. The optimistic night nurse said, "He really didn't have a very good night." Coming from her I know it was actually really bad.

Finding it harder and harder to stay positive but I just gotta believe there's a new Bob waiting to come back to us. PRAY!

AS OF 8:30 AM...

Right now, Bob's body is fully oxygenated at 100% and his ICP is at 15. His blood pressure looks good and he's breathing normally (well, normal for him on a vent). He tolerated everything this morning with no raise in pressure...this is a very positive thing! The nurse let me take part in his care, which was actually really scary. He has too many tubes and wires and stuff. I was afraid I was going to break him :) She told me not to worry because if I did anything I wasn't supposed to, I would set off alarms and bells and whistles. Thankfully, all remained quiet. So, at 5AM this morning I was in the dumps and couldn't even bring myself to think about what today would bring and now at 9AM I'm helping with his care and all his numbers look good. Geez! Seriously? This is sooooo crazy!

AS OF 10:30 AM

Did CT last night. Brain looks good. In fact, the small little bruises have cleared up and swelling has gone down. She said CT looked good!!!!! YAYAYAYAYAYAYAY!!!!! Brain is stabilizing. Now it's the secondary stuff. We have to watch the lung issue and keep an eye on his right arm. Might have a circulation issue. Doing ultra sound to find out.

SUNDAY, FEBRUARY 20, 3:30 PM

All is well. Still calm and quiet. We prayed for a boring day and we got a boring day, thank goodness. There was a really comfy chair in one of the empty rooms so I confiscated it and put it in Bob's room. Since I can sit with him now without affecting his recovery, I might just as well be comfortable. In fact, it was so comfortable I woke myself up snoring. :)

Sunday night and all is calm. Just spoke with the nurse and Bob is "perfectly boring." Woo hoo! Let's pray for a boring night so we can all get some rest for a change. Good night.

LUCKY DAY 13

Monday February 21, 2011 As of right now, Bob had a relatively quiet night. He had a spike in ICP up into the 40s but by the time the doc was called, ICP was back in the teens. I don't know if that's anything to worry about or not. I just constantly worry at this point so I'll add it to the list. Good news — 24 hours ago he was being ventilated with 100% oxygen because of the lung issues. This was slowly reduced over the last day and he is now at 70%. Woo hoo! I don't really know what that means but I know they don't like to vent at 100% and the sooner they can reduce it, the better. So far, he's tolerating the reduction and his body is staying oxygenated. Today an ultra sound will be done on his right arm to see what's causing the swelling. I also need to ask where we are on all the other meds. I've been so focused on lungs and arms I just let the medical team take care of the drugs. Praying HARD for another calm day.

GOOD NEWS ON DAY 13

Ultra sound of right arm shows all clear; no blood clot. Will elevate to help with fluid retention. Oxygen level and ICP still look good today. Waiting to talk with Neuro doc to get update on drugs and maybe an idea of what's next. I don't have the energy for a hard day so Bob is cooperating nicely. I decided it's all about me today...me, me, me. :) Ha!

BTW: Neuro doc said we will continue this course and just give Bob more time. PRAYING HARD AND LOUD that Bob has a calm night so I don't receive a phone call at home and have to fly back to the hospital. Driving nearly 100 mph on dry roads is one thing. Driving that fast tonight would be truly insane.

END OF LUCKY DAY 13

We're ending our day on a good note. Bob's ICP is 12 and his oxygen level is where it needs to be. I sure hope he rests comfortably and continues doing what he's doing. Could this be a turning point? I guess we'll "wait and see" (That's what everyone keeps saying here. It's like their mantra or something).

TUESDAY, FEBRUARY 22, DAY 14

During the night, ICP spiked over 40 but came back down with drugs. I spoke with nurse early this morning and she said there was really no change except for the spike. He did that Sunday night too and Monday early afternoon. Day nurse said she's giving him "lots" of extra sedative to keep ICP down. Not sure what that means. Is it good that he's having "burst suppressions" on his EEG? I have no idea. Nurse said that's good but it means he's only lightly sedated. Is that good at this point? I don't know but I can tell ya I'm not talking with any trauma drama docs. Those guys are just plain scary mean...and a$$e$. Their egos are bigger than Texas! Granted, they work on brains for a living so they have a right but geez, getta grip on your people skills, people!! Perhaps I will take out a trauma doc today. That would make ME feel better :) On second thought, maybe I'll just wait and talk with a Neuro doc.

LUNCH TIME

I'm actually hungry today. Neuro doc says we may increase sedation to keep ICP down. There's a big balancing act going on right now between the brain and the body. What's good for one isn't necessarily good for the other. They want to get

Bob off the vent and put in a trach but they also need to make sure ICP stabilizes. My understanding is they don't do a trach if he's on Pentobarb. Also might change pressure monitor just to make sure it's accurately reading the ICP. More waiting around to see what happens this afternoon.

ALL'S CALM TODAY

ICP hit an all time low of 7 today. Haven't seen that number since way last week sometime. Woo hoo! Could it be that he's actually getting his head in the game now? :) Nurse told me today he's a medical mystery. ICP should only be fluctuating if brain is swelling. However, CT scan shows swelling is reduced from last week and small pinpoint bruises have healed. Perhaps that supports the doc's theory that the monitor is not registering correctly? Hmmmm...I think I would prefer all the equipment work properly when it comes to Bob's brain. When Bob has good days, I have good days and then I eat too much. I had half a bag of cookies (aka about 50# of sugar) and now I have a stomach ache. I'm like a little kid that doesn't know when to stop. Could that be why I'm talking so fast and not able to sit still? I expect to have a sugar crash soon.

REFLECTIONS ON 2 WEEKS PAST

2 weeks ago today at 6:30 pm our lives changed forever. We are truly and exceptionally blessed to have so much support from family, friends, coworkers and even people we don't know. On Monday morning after the horrible ice storm, a nice man in the hotel parking lot helped me scrape my car. It made me cry. I'm sure he thought I was loony but he has no idea how much that meant to me.

All of the cards, letters, gifts and well wishes are sincerely appreciated and all of you are helping us thru this with your positive thoughts, prayers and great support. The human spirit is alive and well all around us and for that we are truly grateful. THANK YOU!

WEDNESDAY, FEBRUARY 23, DAY 15

It's a good thing the nurses put the date on the white board in Bob's room or I would have no idea.

Stable all night. ICP jumped when they did chest x-ray but whose wouldn't?! They put this big metal plate behind him and it looks incredibly uncomfortable. Other than that, he's behaving rather nicely. Putting arterial line in arm today (moving it from his femoral artery). Also still talking about a trach but they need to get him off the Pentobarb b/4 doing trach. So many things to balance at this point! Another day of procedures and things to watch. Pray all goes well. It scares me when they start messin' with him. It would be great if they could just let him be but he has to have this stuff so he can heal. Praying all goes well today!

WEDNESDAY EVENING, FEBRUARY 23

Ahhhh...another calm day. Bob is resting comfortably. They planned to do a trach this afternoon but the medical team was doing other things. I'm fine with waiting until tomorrow. Bob needs another calm night before we rile him up again. Possibility they may still do one tonight but the nurses felt they would probably wait until tomorrow. Makes me nervous and I'm adding it to my worry list. I'm hoping to cross things off my worry list soon. :0

MORNING OF DAY 16

Doing trach right now. Also putting feeding tube directly into his stomach now. Scared! Praying Bob handles these procedures well. They do them right in the room and the nurse said, "I know it sounds scary but we do these all the time." He's still on Pentobarb so I guess they can do a trach and feeding tube while he's on this. Today is freakin' me out a little. I'm sure I'll relax a bit after these are done and he's resting comfortably.

Trach's done and feeding tube is in...yay! Bob tolerated everything with flying colors. His ICP only spiked to 17 and now it's back down. Doc said he did better than she thought he would and she said he's finally getting with the program :) Woo hoo!

Here's an amazing thing - Bob always uses dental picks and keeps them in his mouth. They found his dental pick in his THROAT!!!!! It's been there for 16 days. Thank goodness it didn't perforate anything or slip down his airway. In fact, they were quite glad they did the trach and got that thing outta there! Life lesson for everyone - DON'T LEAVE TOOTH PICKS IN YOUR MOUTH EVER. That's directly from the doc and given this experience, I'm never even using a tooth pick again.

END OF DAY 16

All is well as we come to the end of Day 16. Neuro doc even talked about possibly removing the pressure monitor and reducing more drugs this weekend. She even started talking about rehab. This is the first time I've heard anyone mention anything about the future...woo hoo! I'm confident we've made it over the first big hurdle. Bob still has a lot going on and a lot to watch - antibiotic for lungs, blood clot in leg, potential skin issues. Now we have to see what this weekend will bring. Time, time and more time. We'll just have to "wait and see." I still pack an overnight bag every day just in case.

HAPPY FRIDAY! FEBRUARY 25, DAY 17

Bob is resting comfortably. I sat with him for awhile this morning and his ICP was 0 at one point. Can you believe it? That's the same as you and me!!!!

Ran into another doc and he said that Bob made it over the hump. What a great thing to hear. Now it's just time and waiting and managing the drugs. Today and this weekend will see more subtle changes. Waiting to see how these changes will affect Bob.

I'm such a nervous norkus these days. Anytime they do something, I freak out a little. His numbers are so good right now I want to just leave him alone for a minute. They did a lot of stuff to him yesterday and want him to have a nice calm day today.

FRIDAY AFTERNOON

Bob keeps breathing over his vent, which means he takes an extra breath now and then on his own. It totally freaks me out. The vent makes this honking noise and then I get nervous. They're going to give him something to make him a bit more relaxed so that doesn't happen. The extra breath is also making his blood pressure go up and his heart rate to be elevated. Hope he balances out and calms down a little.

END OF DAY 17

All's quiet tonight. Problems with elevated blood pressure and heart rate but it's to be expected as they back off the sedation meds. Controlling it with yet more drugs. Interesting that Bob went to his cardiologist just the day before the accident and he was healthy enough to stop taking his blood pressure meds. He also doesn't have to go back to the cardiologist for 2 years now. Good to know his heart is strong. He is still breathing over his vent once in awhile, which makes the vent honk. One of my friends said the vent is honking to get back at me for snoring in his room. Ha! Made me laugh so I had to share :) It's good to laugh. BTW - thank you to the nice neighbor, whoever you are, that snow blowed the drive and walkway on Weds or Thurs (still having a problem remembering what day it is). Sure was great to come home and not have to shovel!

SATURDAY, FEBRUARY 26, DAY 18

BOB IS FLUTTERING HIS EYES!!!!! Holy crap. :) GO BOB!

The doc can't believe that he's doing that already given all the pain and anti-anxiety meds he's on. He's already startin' to wake up! The nurse told me to start talkin with him so I did and his ICP shot up to 40. Scared the crap out of me so I backed out of the room and it went back to 8. I think I'll talk to him every couple of hours or so. He's probably trying to tell me to quit being such a worry wart and cry baby. So here's what's next, as long as Bob tolerates these changes:

> 3% sodium is done - that was the stuff to get the fluid off the brain. Pentobarb will be done Monday. Versed for anxiety and Phentinol for pain (probably not spelled correctly) will slowly be lowered as he can tolerate them. He will be heavily sedated yet so won't know really how awake he is on his own because he'll still be drugged. Probably a couple of weeks yet before we know how awake the new Bob will be. GO BOB!!!!

EVENING OF SATURDAY, DAY 18

As they reduce the sedation, it takes Bob awhile to adjust so he needs extra injections of meds to calm down a little. He was really fighting the vent for awhile and trying to breathe over it. A little shot of extra sedation and he's all calm again.

Every time I sit with him, he starts to wake up. He blinks his eyes, his heart rate goes up and so does his blood pressure and then he starts breathing over the vent. It's not like I'm being all lovey dovey or anything. I was just telling him about the weather for Pete sake. Geez, calm down, man. Maybe I SHOULD be all mushy. :)

SUNDAY, FEBRUARY 27, DAY 19

Again...so glad the nurse puts the day and date on the white board. I would have bet the farm today was Monday!

Bob's having a rather up and down day today. Settings on vent were changed to allow Bob to breathe more on his own but blood pressure is an issue and his heart rate is up. They think he's doing that "storming" thing again. From what I heard from the doc, storming is common in severe traumatic head injuries and happens as the sedation is reduced. Controlling the symptoms and extra shots of sedation will get him through. I just gotta believe he's brainstorming his way back to us. More praying, waiting and watching today.

SUNDAY NIGHT

Well...I'm not sure what the next days have in store. Bob's blood pressure, heart rate, breathing, and temperature are an issue. It's all part of the "storming." Right now, these things are being controlled with drugs. Apparently, this could go on for many days, even weeks. I'm not sure I can handle weeks of this. The nurse reassured me that this is common and Bob is getting one-on-one care because he has so much going on. I'm hoping I can sleep tonight at least for a little bit. It will be a long day of watching numbers and waiting tomorrow. Pray the drugs keep working!

MONDAY, FEBRUARY 28, DAY 20

Rough night for Bob. ICP and blood pressure very high. Had to restart the 3%. We're going backwards. Doc concerned that 3 weeks out from the accident, we are still dealing with cranial pressure. Doc also said Bob seems to be doing whatever he wants...which would be OK with me if he would just do whatever he wants in the right direction! Long day today. I'm all nerves again. Praying that Bob comes around soon!

MONDAY AFTERNOON

Just spoke with Physician's Assistant for Neuro.

Very nice and had all positive things to say. She says Neuro and Trauma doc (the good trauma doc) who have been working the case are encouraged and feel like Bob is moving in the right direction from when he first arrived. I told you most of these trauma docs are scary (aka evil!). Trauma doc from this morning had me all nervous again...geez! Right now, the drugs are managing Bob's issues so he'll just continue to work thru this. Could be awhile yet before he's completely off drugs but time we have to give so not a problem. Maybe I can sleep well tonight with this news. Sure hope so.

MARCH 2011

TUESDAY, MARCH 1, DAY 21

Holy crap it's March! What the heck happened to February? :)

Good news first - in response to pain, Bob moved his RIGHT side and opened his eyes and blinked normally for about 2 minutes last night! That's HUGE considering the most damage was done to the left side of his brain. Left side brain affects right side body. Also, he's on so much Fentynol and Versed it's astonishing he's reacting at all. If you've ever taken a pain pill, you know how those can make you loopy. Well, he's on mega-horse doses of those things and he's still reacting, which is GOOD. Woo hoo! GO BOB! Blood pressure is still an issue but they are trying drugs like Enderol and Ketal-something (I can't remember all the drug names) to keep pressure under control. So far it's still high so that will be a battle for today. He's also running a fever and his lungs are getting cloudy again. Keeping an eye on all this stuff and managing the ups and downs. I'm going to make a point of eating more. Rice cakes and corn chex are boring! :)

TUESDAY AFTERNOON, STILL MARCH 1, DAY 21

Now he has blood clots in his arms from not moving. Vascular team is coming up to review and see what needs to be done. Yet another team of doctors...oh yippee! These guys better talk to me or else...I'll kick 'em in the shins and run. Started a low dose of blood thinner this morning (it's like heparin but not heparin). His bed is back on rotation but he really doesn't like it. His ICP hangs out in the teens and his blood pressure hangs out in the high 160s when the bed is on but he needs to have the bed on rotation to prevent blood clots and skin deterioration. Oy! One thing leads to another.

Tuesday night and all is calm. Bob opened his eyes and blinked for about 30 seconds. He had just been moved around a little and it made him a little more "awake." He was breathing heavy from that little bit of activity so I told him to rest and he closed his eyes and his breathing calmed down! GO BOB!

It was 3 weeks ago today that these terrible set of circumstances all came together to put us in this situation. We've been on the worst roller coaster ride EVER. The ups and downs are horrendous. We pray, we cry, we hope, we laugh...some days all in the same hour! With the support of everyone around us, we've made it this far and continue down the path to recovery. Bob is making progress and I'm confident that he is strong enough, determined enough, and undoubtedly handsome enough to make it through this. For that we are truly grateful.

WEDNESDAY, MARCH 2, DAY 22

Bob's baby blues are open and blinking normally. Actually, he looks wasted. Ha! He's still gettin' the really good drugs. :) He's having some breathing issues today, which makes me a nervous wreck. I'm on my last nerve. I never really knew what that meant until now. know I wouldn't describe myself as a nervous person but, MAN, I guess that changed! I jump at every noise...geez! AHHH! The nurse said he's fully oxygenated and his breathing isn't an issue for him so he's OK. It's just me.

WEDNESDAY AFTERNOON

Bob's going to have a filter put in tomorrow to prevent clots from traveling anywhere they shouldn't (Greenfield filter). "Simple" procedure and takes around 10 minutes. Docs are confident he'll tolerate it just fine. I, on the other hand, will be a nervous wreck again I'm sure. Maybe I'll skip my morning coffee tomorrow.

THURSDAY, MARCH 3, DAY 23

Haven't seen Bob yet today. He had his filter procedure this morning. All went fine. Hope to see him soon. When they wheeled him by he looked good and resting comfortably. Praying for a calm day and that the procedure didn't rile him up at all.

THURSDAY AFTERNOON, STILL DAY 23

Because of the sedation for the procedure this morning, Bob is out of it. New medical term - doc says Bob is "schnokered." He'll probably sleep the rest of the day, which is fine with me. He's all settled in and looks peaceful. Will be removing some of the many gadgets he required when he first got here (temperature regulator, one IV line, no more EEG). His need for a lot of stuff is shrinking. YAY! GO BOB!

THURSDAY NIGHT, DAY 23

Still stable. Those beautiful baby blues were open for about an hour this evening and then he went back to sleep. Now that the Arctic Sun (temperature regulator) has been removed, his temp is creeping up. Tylenol should keep it in check but if not, then the Arctic Sun will go back on. The Arctic Sun is this really ingenious machine. It involves these blue pads that go on Bob's arms, legs and body. Water is pumped thru the pads and either cools or warms depending on his body temperature. Who comes up with these things? They deserve a medal! Two new technical terms today - "Schnokered" and "gobble-de-gook." Doc said Bob was "schnokered" after his sedation this morning and nurse said she put "gobble-de-gook" on his eyes to keep them moist. Ha! Now those are words I can understand.

TGIF! MARCH 4, DAY 24

Well...the Arctic Sun is back on but it's controlling Bob's temp so that's good. Talking about taking the pressure monitor out. That's a HUGE step forward. After that's out, we can start lowering the other meds and even start some physical therapy. Hoping and praying this weekend we have some progress in the right direction. GO BOB!

FRIDAY AFTERNOON, DAY 24

Woo hoo! Bob doesn't need his pressure monitor anymore. It's gone! Yay! Neuro doc says, "He's gettin' better." Blood pressure, heart rate, and respirations are all fine right now. Still watching temp. He was "awake" for just a short time today and now resting comfortably. GO BOB!

FRIDAY NIGHT

Not much new tonight. Bob had his eyes open for just a short time today but still not quite ready to focus. He's still pretty drugged up. Starting to lower some of the meds so we should see some progress in the next few days. Praying for positive progress at whatever pace Bob requires. We'll wait as long as it takes!

SATURDAY MORNING, MARCH 5, DAY 25

Chest x-ray looks better! YAY! Changed vent settings so Bob is breathing more on his own. It's hard to watch again. He takes these really deep breaths and kind of holds them in. I have to remember to breathe when I sit with him. Also lowered the meds and he's tolerating that just fine so far. Hope to see those baby blues again today. It would be great if he squeezed my hand too but I'm trying not to rush things. Ha! You'd think after 25 days I would learn some patience! I'm getting sick of this waiting room. Would really like to see some progress so we can move to another floor.

SATURDAY AFTERNOON

Good day for Bob. He must like cold rainy days. He got a new bed. He doesn't need the big blow-up mattress thingy anymore. He looks a lot more comfortable. Maybe the swelling in his arms will go down now, too. His forearms are bigger than his legs!

I haven't seen him "awake" today but Mike told him golf season is almost here and his eyes popped WIDE open. It's time to put some golf pictures up in his room. GO BOB!

SATURDAY EVENING, MARCH 5, DAY 25

Bob finally had his eyes open for me while I was sitting with him. He's not quite ready to focus yet but I gotta believe he's trying! He still has a lot of drugs floating thru his system. Speaking of drugs, the Fentynol is now down to just a patch instead of a drip...one less IV. WOO HOO! The Versed is quite high yet but that's coming down too and Bob's tolerating all of this just fine. Even after they turn down (or off) the drugs, it still takes awhile for them to flush out of his system so the nurses don't expect to see a lot of progress yet. I'm not worried (yea, right). My worry list is still rather long :)

Thank you for all of the continued thoughts, prayers and support. My cousin's church in Amsterdam, Netherlands, is now praying as well so we truly have support from all over the world!

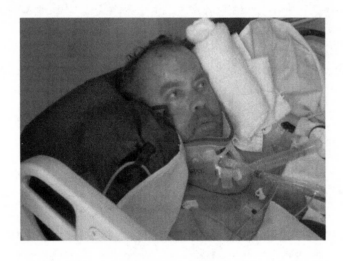

SUNDAY, MARCH 6, DAY 26

Bob's down for his MRI right now so haven't seen him yet. I'm not sure how long it will take to get the results but I hope it's soon. Would really like to know what the doc has to say after the MRI. Unfortunately, I think I'll be dealing with the trauma drama team more now. Pray for THEIR safety. HA! :)

SUNDAY NIGHT, DAY 26

Results of MRI show that Bob has a brain injury...well, DUH! Basically he has the same type of injuries as shaken baby syndrome. Same information we knew nearly 4 weeks ago when this first happened. We haven't talked with the trauma dramas yet but will tomorrow. He did have his eyes open before we left tonight and I swear he looked at me and followed my face while I was in front of his line of vision. I thought I saw him do that yesterday, too. I hope I'm not dreaming and being overly optimistic. I'm going to wear really bright colors tomorrow so I will either make him close his eyes or he'll follow me around the room. I'm thinking a nice bright orange hunters cap. I will be so gorgeous it's scary :)

MONDAY, MARCH 7, DAY 27

Yay! Bob now has a schedule for physical therapy and occupational therapy. They will be moving his arms and legs and making him do some stuff now. His eyes were wide open this morning. He looks really good. Arm swelling has gone down and blood pressure is stable. I'm not talking to the docs yet because they will burst my bubble (more like squash and stomp all over my bubble!).

Bob's room is really tiny but we're going to try and sit in there as much as possible without getting in the way of his care. I was reading the new Golf Digest articles to him this morning and he kept yawning. I didn't realize I was so boring :)

MONDAY NIGHT, MARCH 7, DAY 27

Bob no longer needs the respirator and he's breathing on his own!!! YAY! He still has the trach but this is the next big step. Woo Hoo! Each day brings little positive points of progress. Look forward to seeing what tomorrow will bring. GO BOB!!!

TUESDAY, MARCH 8, DAY 28

Bob is having an awesome day today. He is on a schedule for therapy with 2 hours activity and 2 hours of quiet. Today they had him sitting up! Amazing! The bed he's on is called a Sports Bed and it bends into a chair. It's the coolest thing. They just push a couple buttons and...voila...he's sitting up. His blood pressure, respirations and heart rate all stayed fine during the whole thing. That's another amazing thing because you'd expect his blood pressure to tank after lying still for 4 weeks and then all of a sudden sitting up. Therapy team and nurse were amazed at how well he did. He has to wear a back brace when they sit him up because of the compression fracture in his lower back. It takes them longer to get him set up in that than it does to actually do his therapy. We are talking with the docs tonight so I'll find out more about his lower back injury. Lots of progress today!!!! :) GO BOB!

ONE MONTH AGO TODAY...

Wow, the things that can happen in a month! It was 4 weeks ago tonight that all this craziness started. Up, down, up, down...and then up again. The progress Bob has made in just the past 3 days is amazing. Now that therapy started, the family can take part in his care. What a HUGE difference that makes for all of us, including Bob. He's making slow and steady progress and we'll keep giving him more time. Thank you for all the support, prayers, well wishes, and positive thoughts. They're working!!!!

WEDNESDAY, MARCH 9, DAY 29

Happy Birthday Mom (aka Shirley)! It's quiet time now so Bob is resting but at noon we'll get him up again and see what he will do for mom's birthday. The people from rehab stopped by today and talked about when he might be able to move. Could be this week! Holy crap! :) GO BOB!

WEDNESDAY EVENING, MARCH 9, DAY 29

Yep, that's right...tomorrow Bob's moving to a Long Term Acute Care Hospital (LTACH). The healthcare field has more acronyms than the government! The LTACH is called Borgess-PIP. It's a stepping stone between critical care and rehab. Bob still has the need for a respirator at night and he still needs some drugs so PIP will be able to manage his medical needs and start his therapy. Sleep well, Bob, because tomorrow will be a big day!

WOO HOO! GO BOB GO!

BTW: I was standing at the foot of his bed and called his name. He opened his eyes and followed me from one corner of the room to the other! That's called tracking and it's the first time he's done it without me putting myself in his line of vision first. That's a huge WOO HOO for Bob!

THURSDAY, MARCH 10, DAY 30

Happy Birthday, Mom (aka Nita Anne)! Nope, this isn't deja vu. Both moms have birthdays just one day apart. Sorry, Bob and I didn't send cards this year but we promise to send 2 next year. :) Bob's not leaving today. His white cell count is elevated and his liver enzymes are funky so they think it's his gull bladder. Doing ultra sound at 4pm this afternoon to find out. Doc said it's quite common given all the drugs he's had the past 4 weeks. She also said it's done lapriscopicly so minimally invasive (wow, those are some nice medical words). We're OK with him staying here for a few days. We're looking at this as just a plateau rather than a set back. It's just a little hitch in his giddy-up that's all.

THURSDAY EVENING

Well crap. Bob is having gall (not gull) bladder surgery tomorrow morning at 7:30 am. Apparently, he had gall stones but didn't have any symptoms (at least not that I'm aware of). All the things that helped him in the past 4 weeks made his gall bladder bad. Pray they can do this lapariscopically. The recovery is much easier and faster. If the surgery is done in the traditional way, then we'll be at Borgess for another 1-1/2 to 2 weeks.

We know the road to recovery is going to be long and bumpy but really? I don't like the bumps! (Please forgive all my spelling issues. I type too fast and end up spelling things how they sound)

FRIDAY, MARCH 11, DAY 31

GO BOB Central here. All's well. Bob's out of surgery and back in his room already. All went well and they removed the gall bladder laparoscopically (I think that's spelled correctly now). For some reason it was smashed up against his colon. Eeewww. Just the thought of that is disgusting. I'm not sure where the gall bladder is in relationship to the colon but I'm pretty sure they're not supposed to be smashed together. He is resting comfortably and may be going to Borgess-PIP (the LTACH) on Monday. Woo hoo! New surroundings for us and a new plan for Bob. GO BOB!

FRIDAY NIGHT, DAY 31

Bob had a "light" therapy session this afternoon and he shows muscle tone and movement on his right side. COOL! The next step is to get him to squeeze a hand. Repetition, repetition, repetition. I know this sounds bad but it's easier for some patients to stick out their tongues at first because moving a hand or foot is too much. So, I walk around all day saying, "Bob, stick out your tongue" at the top of my lungs. I might be scaring small children at this point. We decided that Bob earned points for "Most Creative" with his little gall bladder stunt. He's full of surprises so, as brother Bruce says, "Keep your lap bar down until the ride comes to a full and complete stop!" Get ready for tomorrow. Who knows what's next. :)

SATURDAY, MARCH 12, DAY 32

Happy Birthday, brother Jack! I think that's the last of the March birthdays for the family. No fever and blood pressure/ heart rate are fine this morning. Getting rid of that gnarly ol' gall bladder must have done the trick. During our 2 hours of activity this morning, Bob stayed "awake" for about an hour and a half. I threatened to read the golf digest articles again and he opened his eyes...HA! :) He's more "awake" in the afternoon so we'll see what happens this afternoon. "BOB, stick out your tongue."

SUNDAY, MARCH 13, DAY 33
LUCKY NUMBER 13

Bob's body clock is off an hour today...and so is mine. I swear it takes me a week to get used to the time change. Hopefully, he adjusts better than I do. I'm 100% positive he moved his head!!!! The nurses are skeptical but I know what I saw. He's lying on his left side and I was talking in his right ear. I know he moved his head because his cheek was resting on his neck brace and he picked it up. It wasn't a little move either. It was him turning his head towards my voice. I'm going to start video taping this stuff. Now, if we can just get him to..."BOB, stick out your tongue." GO BOB!

SUNDAY AFTERNOON

We'll be staying at Borgess for a few days yet. Low grade fever and elevated white cell count. Somewhere there is an infection. Starting antibiotics today and are doing cultures of lungs to see if they can figure out what bug is causing the problem. They're not even sure it's the lungs. We're OK with Bob staying here as long as it takes to make sure he's stable and ready for therapy. However, I must say I was looking forward to the solarium at the new place (they call the waiting room the "solarium" and it's beautiful with 2 full walls of windows, recliners and a big screen TV - and it has FREE coffee!). And Bob's room will be pretty nice, too.

MONDAY, MARCH 14, DAY 34

Bob looks well rested today. He wasn't too excited about being "awake" this morning so I turned on the Rolling Stones and we rocked out the 7th floor. I really look like a crazy person jumpin' around to the music but it keeps Bob interested. My hair is really long and it sticks out on the sides, which doesn't help. I think I scared the cleaning guy! :) Tomorrow we should know what type of antibiotics Bob needs to clear up his low grade fever and high white cell count. Pray this is a simple easy fix and he's back on his way to rehab. GO BOB!

MONDAY EVENING

GREAT DAY TODAY! During therapy, Bob had a normal reaction to pain (he pulled away instead of pushing into it) AND he held his head up by himself. I told you he moved his head yesterday. Even though I dance around like a mad woman, I'm really not crazy. The cleaning guy might think otherwise. Figured out the source of infection and what the bug is so started antibiotics this afternoon. We should be headed for Borgess-PIP on Wednesday but don't tell Bob or he'll come up with another outlandish reason to stay. He certainly is creative.

Little positive things for us but great big gains for Bob. GO BOB! And as one of my corny friends said, "PIP-PIP-Hurray"! :)

TUESDAY, MARCH 15, DAY 35

No fever today! YAY! Antibiotics are working. He also moved his head again this morning. So exciting to see reactions and great to see his baby blues open and alert. There's talk of moving Bob today but nurse said, "I don't know anything yet." I said, "Well, hasn't that been my life for the past 5 weeks?" So here we sit patiently waiting for what's next. :)

TUESDAY, 2 HOURS LATER

WE'RE GOING TO BORGESS PIP AT 3:00 TODAY! WOO HOO! GO BOB!

Last night, doc said Bob might leave here Weds if antibiotics were working and not to plan on leaving Tuesday. As of

10 this morning, still hadn't heard anything about moving. At 10:30, doc stopped by and said they needed to do MRI of Bob's neck before he could leave so that meant he wouldn't leave here until Thursday. At 12:00, we were told that Bob is moving TODAY at 3:00. And that pretty much sums up the way our lives have been for the past 5 weeks. Every day is another surprise in more ways than one! GO BOB!

FIVE WEEKS AGO TODAY, THIS CRAZY RIDE STARTED

What an adventure. Never in our wildest dreams could we imagine our lives the way they've been since February 8. 5 weeks in the Neuro-Critical Unit (NCU), one less gall bladder and now a new room at Borgess-Pipp. Today we start Phase 2. Bob will have concentrated therapy 6 days a week. Not sure what that involves but I'm sure we'll know soon enough. Praying and praying for more positive improvements. Keep the faith and keep praying! GO BOB GO!

WEDNESDAY, MARCH 16, DAY 36

WE HAVE TONGUE PEOPLE! I'm not sure it was on command but at least we know he's capable! WOO HOO! I will continue my repetitive chant, "Bob, stick out your tongue" until I'm positive he does it on command. At some point, he will probably just do it when he sees me to keep me quiet! GO BOB!

WEDNESDAY NIGHT, DAY 36

We celebrate the good and we plow thru the not-so-good. Because Bob has an infection and he had his aortic valve replaced with a pig valve 3 years ago, they had to do an echocardiogram to make sure the bacteria has not affected the valve. We will have the test results tomorrow. Please pray for a clear and readable echocardiogram. If it isn't readable, then it's back to the hospital for a TEE(transesophageal echocardiogram). If the tests show the valve has bacteria, then it's a course of antibiotics for 6 weeks and we pray they work! I believe the tests are precautionary to make sure nothing is missed so keep praying and thinking positive. Right now, he's resting comfortably in his beautiful new room at Pipp.

THURSDAY, MARCH 17, DAY 37

Happy St Patty's Day! I look sick in green and I didn't want to be mistaken for a patient so you're all allowed to pinch me today. Big therapy session this morning. Bob's worn out. Talking about sitting him up on the edge of the bed maybe this afternoon but for sure tomorrow. The goal is to retrain his brain (remapping). Repeat after me, "Bob, stick out your tongue." Still waiting for results of echocardiogram from yesterday. Hope and pray all is well. GO BOB!

THURSDAY EVENING, DAY 37

Well, the echo looked good but as suspected, they couldn't see the valves on the underside of the heart. It's back to the hospital tomorrow for the TEE (transesophageal echocardiogram). This is a precautionary measure to make sure there isn't bacteria on the valve. Bob has to be at the hospital at 11am and the TEE will be at 1pm so it's another ambulance ride to and from the hospital. Plus he'll have more sedation so we'll be a day or two behind on therapy. If there is bacteria on the valve, then it will be a 6 week course of antibiotics. Please, Lord, let this be the last thing so we can set a course for rehab and start recovery.

THURSDAY NIGHT, DAY 37

I don't know why I'm still up but alas, sleep is out of my reach tonight. I had to research the cardiologist - Dr. Gustafson, ya, from Minnesota, aye. He's 45 and been practicing for 17 years, dontchya know, and he works up there to the hospital. Yer darn tootin'! I'll try not to laugh and use my silly Minnesota accent tomorrow when I talk with him. I apologize now to friends and family in Minnesota but you know I tease you because I love you :)

FRIDAY, MARCH 18, DAY 38

TEE went well. No signs of bacteria on the heart valves and Bob tolerated the ride and the procedure just fine. He had Versed and increased Fentynol so he's "schnokered" again. Sound asleep. The sedation they use is similar to what you get when you have a colonoscopy so he should be awake in a little while. From what I understand, Bob's white cell count went from 21 on Sunday to 14 on Wednesday and back up to 16 on Thursday. Waiting for doc so he can explain what's next. If white cells are going up again but Bob's on antibiotic, then what changed? Is he on the right antibiotic? Is the pig valve still in jeopardy because the bacteria is still in his system? Oy, so many questions.

BOB SQUEEZED MY HAND! It was a big squeeze too, not some mamby pamby "did he or didn't he" but a big turn-my-thumb-red squeeze. The physical therapist saw it too confirming that I'm not crazy!!!! I don't know what they did during the TEE but whatever it was they need to keep doing it. Bob was wide awake from about 1:30 to 3:00 so we took advantage of it and did some therapy (and he squeezed my hand). He's superman. Both the pulmonologist and the internist suggest a ride everyday. Good, fresh, outdoor air woke him up! I said write the order and let's do it (so he can squeeze my hand everyday). As far as bacteria, we're going to continue the course of treatment with current antibiotic and review daily blood cultures. Head trauma could be affecting white cell count. At least the heart valves are clean so one less thing to worry about.

This was a big day for Bob, going back and forth to the hospital, having sedation and then moving his arms and hands (and squeezing my hand). We know that he may be tired and sleep all day tomorrow but today was HUGE! ...and did I mention that BOB SQUEEZED MY HAND! GO BOB!

SATURDAY, MARCH 19, DAY 39

Bob was actually mellow today – no surprises. He was coughing a bit but everyone says that's good and he has a really strong cough. Now we're supposed to encourage him to swallow after he coughs to start working on his swallowing ability. Yuck! That gives me the heebee jeebees but if it's good for Bob, then I'll get over it...eeewwww, gross! That just made me shiver. I guess I'm not over it yet. He had his eyes open on and off most of the afternoon. I leave in the evenings when he falls asleep but he just wanted to hang out and be awake so I sat with him until about 8pm. It was pretty warm in his room so I repositioned the pillows and made sure the fan was blowing around him and he fell asleep. He probably opened his eyes as soon as I was gone and stuck out his tongue :)

White cell count is down to 12 (normal is 6 to 10.8). Let's hope that pesky infection is finally going away. Should know for sure tomorrow or Monday. Thanks for all of the prayers, positive thoughts and continued support.

SUNDAY, MARCH 20, DAY 40

Today Bob's blood pressure is an issue. It's around 170/60. They had to switch the IV twice in his right hand and now they're using a bigger needle. OUCH! My blood pressure would be up, too. White cell count is down to 11. YAY! That means Vancomycin is working and infection is leaving. Will keep monitoring blood cultures to make sure this extra little thing is fixed now too. So to recap the extras, Bob had gall bladder attack, mild pneumonia and then bacteremia. Gall bladder is gone, pneumonia is gone and bacteremia is on its way out. Nurses at Borgess NCU said that the brain was first and we can fix the secondary stuff later. Now, let's hope the secondary stuff is fixed so we can set a course for recovery and a plan for rehab! GO BOB!

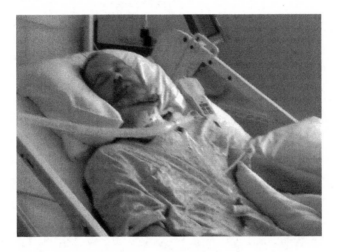

SUNDAY EVENING, DAY 40

Bob moved his head! Can you imagine how heavy his head feels to him? He actually turned his head to see what he was missing on his other side. It was so good to see him do that in response to sound and commotion. He also continues to move his arms in response to touch and grips my hand with his left hand. It will be an absolute miracle when he's able to actually lift them up. I will dance around with my tongue sticking out! Speaking of tongues, he licked his lips today too. So he can obviously stick out his tongue so guess what I'll be working on tomorrow. :)

I just spoke to the nurse this evening and he's resting comfortably. Blood pressure is good and he was asleep when I called. Phew! Hoping for a restful night. GO BOB!

MONDAY, MARCH 21, DAY 41

Wow! Bob bent his left arm and pulled it up to his stomach. Holy crap it scared me. I jumped about 3 feet. The nurse and I just saw him move his left leg for the first time. When I walked in this morning, the assistant nurse (or whatever they're called now) said that Bob is a lot more responsive today. NICE! He opens his mouth on his own when they brush his teeth. They don't even have to tell him. He just does it. He also gave me the dirtiest look today when I was trying to wake him up. I scratched his beard (which looks like Tom Hanks in Cast Away at this point). It woke him up and then he squeezed my hand. HA! I call that a response to annoyance instead of pain. He also moved every finger on his left hand. GO BOB!!!!! I wonder what he'll do this afternoon.

MONDAY EVENING, DAY 41

The therapists sat Bob up on the side of the bed this afternoon for about 30 seconds. His blood pressure shot up to 193/107... YIKES!!! It took all afternoon to get him comfortable again. He communicates now by squeezing your hand so at least we can ask if he has pain and he can let us know. After some pain meds and some repositioning in the bed, he was sound asleep when I left. It's hard to see someone in pain but the good side of that is he responds to pain by grimacing and squeezing hands so at least he can let us know he has pain. It was a big day for Bob. He did lots of new things so I just sat in his room and stared at him. It probably creeped him out a little but I couldn't help it. It was unbelievable to see him move so much. He holds my hand now (unless he's fast asleep) and it's wonderful to have some interaction again. GO BOB!

TUESDAY, MARCH 22, DAY 42

Bob is so alert now it's wonderful! He was awake from about 6:30 to 10:30 this morning. I think he's sleeping finally. His heart rate goes down and his respirations go down and he looks so peaceful. And then all of a sudden he'll pop open his eyes half way to see what's going on. The speech therapist (Erin) was in this morning and he did everything she asked. He answered all of her questions correctly, too! He was a little upset with us because she just got engaged this weekend so we were laughing and making too much noise. He gave us the evil eye. It's really kinda funny. He does that to all the therapists now. Cracks me up. I sincerely hope he gets mad at them because that means he's engaged and making connections. GO BOB!

SIX WEEKS OF...I CAN'T FIND A WORD TO DESCRIBE IT

Can you believe it's been 6 weeks? I'm not looking back - only looking forward. I can tell you that Bob is amazing. His ability to communicate by squeezing a hand is out-of-this-world magnificent! I still wonder what his first word will be but squeezing my hand is better than words. We have the ability to communicate by using our hands and it's wonderful. 6 weeks is a very small part of a recovery that will take 12 to 18 months and then years to come. We are only just beginning and what a truly fantastic way to start. Prayers, positive thoughts, and support got us this far and will continue to get us through this journey. We are truly blessed by family, friends, coworkers and even people we don't know. We appreciate all the prayers and well wishes. GO BOB GO!

WEDNESDAY, MARCH 23, DAY 43

Happy Birthday, Aunt Helen! Bob is sound asleep right now. They did all kinds of therapy this morning. He responded nicely and now he's tuckered out. They are so nice here. I told them his right side is his comfy side so they always reposition him after therapy so he's laying on this right side. He looks so peaceful. While sitting up in that awful looking hard plastic brace, his blood pressure went up to 190/80 again. That brace looks so uncomfortable they should check MY blood pressure when he's sitting in it. Hopefully the neuro/trauma surgeon will discontinue that thing. Doc here says compression fracture isn't bad. The disc between L1/L2 vertebrae is squished on just the edges. With all the trouble the brace is causing, maybe a girdle would be better or perhaps Bob can borrow a pair of my control top panty hose. Granted, control top panty hose aren't comfortable at all but they are 100% better than that stupid brace!

WEDNESDAY EVENING, DAY 43

Good news! Arms are fine and blood is flowing smoothly through veins and arteries. No more worries there. Blood pressure can now be taken in arms instead of legs. Will give much more accurate reading. YAY!

Not-so-good news...neck brace has to stay on and back brace has to be used when sitting up until Neuro surgeon can take a look. Will take a week or two to see the Neuro doc. This is where I come in. Tomorrow I'll be asking what's delaying the Neuro doc. No way Bob should wait up to 2 weeks to see the doc so they can remove the braces! The neck brace has caused a few red areas from rubbing and the back brace is hindering progress instead of helping. Neuro doc needs to step it up. If Bob still needs the braces, then fine but I'm not leaving the poor man in those braces for 2 weeks just 'cause the Neuro doc is busy. She should know better.

THURSDAY, MARCH 24, DAY 44

Bob was sound asleep this morning until about 10:00. He even slept through most of his range-of-motion therapy (except when they hit a tight spot on his arms and his eyes popped open). About 10:00, they sat him up and he stayed that way for about 30 minutes. His blood pressure was fine but went up to 168/80 after 30 minutes. Still not bad. He's sound asleep again. I knew the leg blood pressures weren't accurate so it's good to be able to take B/P in the arm now. Here's the best part of the day so far - with support from the therapist, Bob will touch his nose, eyes, lips and ears. Because his arms are weak, the therapist will hold them up to his face and he will do everything she asks. That is the most amazing thing I've seen! I cried again. :)

FRIDAY, MARCH 25, DAY 45

BOB SMILED TODAY - a big ol' grin with teeth and smile lines around his eyes. That was the most wonderful thing I've ever seen! The thing is, he smiled like that at the speech pathologist... hmmm...she's petite, cute, bubbly and about 25. 'nuff said. :) Last night, the aides came in to move Bob around and get him more comfortable. When they were done, they asked, "how's that Bob?" and they said he mouthed the word "perfect." The nurse said that head injuries are fascinating because once and awhile, the words will just suddenly come out and then maybe nothing for awhile. A few of the nurses said they've seen him mouth words. I'm still waiting to see that but then I'm fascinated by his hands and legs moving all over so I forget to look at this face, poor guy. That's probably why he smiles and "talks" to the nurses. Here's what I wonder today - when I go home at night, does Bob stick out his tongue, speak to the nurses and then smile because I left? I need to stop being such a wife. I reposition pillows, move around the fan, rub his feet, rub his arms, mess with his beard - I just realized I'm annoying. No wonder he doesn't smile at me!

FRIDAY EVENING, DAY 45

The therapists had Bob sitting on the edge of the bed today. Wow...he was able to sit for about 20 minutes with no blood pressure issues. He's come along way in just the past 5 days. He's doing really well. Doc came in for his daily 3 minutes and Bob just stared at him...again! I'm going to ask the doc to stop in next time the cutey little speech therapist is there. Maybe then the doc will see how well Bob is doing.

One of the patients from Borgess NCU came to Pipp today. It was the other Bob on the floor while our Bob was there. In some weird way, it was nice to see a familiar face. His wife and I became - what's the word? Friends? Confidantes? Partners in head injuries? I don't know. The funny thing is they're right next to each other again. Here we go with the chorus of "Bob, stick out your tongue; Bob, squeeze my hand." These poor Bobs are going to wonder why everyone is named Bob.

SATURDAY, MARCH 26, DAY 46

Bob had a very restful night. So restful he didn't really want to wake up this morning. Finally saw those eyes open about 9:00 am. He did well until about 10:00 and then zonked out again. Who can blame him. He had a foot message, back rub and was repositioned on his comfy side. And guess when the doc came in? Yep, at about 10:20. Figures. Bob's next active time is 12 to 2 so we'll see if we can keep him a little more interested. I saw the Queen of Therapy in the hall this morning. I think she's a director or manager or something. Not sure what they call her but I told her I would like to have a word (I phrased it a bit nicer than that). Haven't seen her yet, which makes me wonder if she's going to work Bob into HER busy schedule today. If not, then that will be 2 days he's missed with his range-of-motion exercises and I will seriously blow a gasket. Still waiting for Dr Eden to call back about neck brace too. Seriously? Doc told me that about 5:30 last night and of course it was too late in the day for me to call. Now I have to wait until Monday. I told the doc this morning about all this so he's aware of my frustration. I was nice about it, even though my tone here isn't very nice :) Stay tuned...

SUNDAY, MARCH 27, DAY 47

Doc stopped by and Bob was awake. Get this...doc asked Bob if he liked the sunshine today and he nodded "YES." HE NODDED YES!!!!! Holy crap! Un-frickin-believable!!!! FINALLY!!!! First time he's even moved for the doc and first time he nodded EVER and he did it for the doc! Perfect timing! I LOVE IT! Can you tell I'm just a little bit excited :) HE NODDED YES!!!! GO BOB! Holy crap again! While I was typing this, nurse came out to tell me Bob was mouthing sentences to her. She couldn't tell what he was saying so she came to get me. I went in and asked if he was comfortable and if he needed anything and he just closed his eyes and fell asleep. I'm going to believe that he was just asking for me, even though nurse couldn't tell what he was saying.

HE'S MOUTHING WORDS!!!!!

Geez! Seriously? I need water proof mascara at this point! :)

I'M STILL EXCITED! :)

He mouthed words to me just a minute ago. I have a picture of us together that I show him all the time. Now it hangs on the bed in his line of sight and I keep telling him it's us in Grand Cayman. He was staring at the pic and then at me and then at the pic. I swear he said, "Grand Cayman." I had to leave for a second (I drank too much coffee) but I'm going back in to stare at Bob some more. :) GO BOB!

MONDAY, MARCH 28, DAY 48

Bob is pooped today. He didn't sleep well last night so quiet times may be a little bit longer today. They did have him sitting on the side of the bed and he moved his left leg. He also shook the therapist's hand and gave her a thumbs up. I, on the other hand, am mad as a hatter. I am now the gestapo when it comes to quiet and awake times. Little insert-bad-name-here nurse's aide came in a few minutes ago and said, "we'd like to get him washed up today" so I told her his next awake time was from 1 to 3. She has the nerve to say to me "well, we'll have to work around our schedule because I have so-and-so that has to take lunch and then I have to take a lunch." I ever so gently reminded her that Bob is on a coma stimulation program and it is essential he has rest periods so from 2 to 3 would be a great time for his bath. insert another bad word here AARRRGGGHHH!!! And...as I'm typing this...in comes EEG tech from Borgess. So much for Bob's restful sleep. For the next hour they'll be messing with him doing the EEG. And yes I'm documenting all this. If any therapist shows up this afternoon and evaluates Bob's stamina, they will see the mad hatter in me! &^%$#@!

MONDAY EVENING, DAY 48

Another good day for Bob. He was tired today, especially after therapy, so we just hung out this afternoon and let him do his thing. He mostly slept but was up a bit in the late afternoon. Should have results of EEG tomorrow. EEG was just to make sure there is no seizure activity going on. Precautionary but let's hope and pray that all is well. Talked with queen therapist and she agreed with everything. I approached it very calmly and nicely and all of my "demands" were met. We're going to try 15 to 20 minutes of therapy for Bob a few times a day instead of 1-1/2 hours all at once. Kinda disappointing that the mad hatter in me didn't have to come out. I guess you really do get further when you're nice instead of mean. Hope I can continue to remember that tomorrow when I get the whole cervical collar issue straightened out.

Rehab is the foundation on which Bob's recovery is based. I will fight whom ever I feel is getting in the way. Bob WILL be the best Bob he can be and we WILL give him the tools he needs to succeed. Look out, I'm on fire! GO BOB!

TUESDAY, MARCH 29, DAY 49

Woo hoo! Bob mouthed words to me again this morning! I'm going to have to practice my lip reading. I'll just pretend he said "Good Morning Cyndi." He slept well last night and was pretty alert this morning. He was in some pain so he just "took" a little Tylenol. Good for therapy this afternoon. Thank goodness Bob is doing so well and making progress in spite of the less than stellar therapy. His medical treatment here is still outstanding and I praise the nurses daily.

No therapy this morning. As a matter of fact, I haven't seen any of the 5 therapists on sight yet today. That blows their agreement to do 2 or 3 shorter sessions of therapy each day. I assume they will be in this afternoon for a full blown 1-1/2 hour session again. I finally got the cervical collar issue straightened out. Not happy the appointment is April 13 but at least I understand what they're going to do and why it is 3 weeks from now. Geez! Took 'em long enough to get that straightened out. Good thing my momma didn't raise no wall flower! :) I've talked to the doc, the queen therapist, the therapists, the nurses, our Borgess-Pipp case manager and today the insurance case manager. NOT HAPPY! Might just as well tell everyone. Mad hatter is really close to the surface today!

TUESDAY AFTERNOON, DAY 49

Holy frickin' moley! BOB JUST SHOOK HIS HEAD AT ME! It's really hot in his room so I put a cold cloth on his head just before rest time. I went in to pick it up and turn it over. I asked if he wanted it on and he almost immediately shook his head no. Holy frickin' moley!!! I tried not to cry because he would think it was stupid to cry over a wash cloth (even though it was the head nod that made me cry) but I couldn't help get tears in my eyes. GO BOB! And get this, the therapist just stopped in and asked Bob for a thumbs up. He did a thumbs up and then spread his fingers and then held up one finger, two fingers, three fingers, and four fingers all on command. He is absolutely 100% capable when he has the rest he needs to expend the energy it takes for the poor guy to move any muscle. I will continue my gestapo-like regime every day. It's working!! GO BOB! (Note to self - start checking pockets again for Kleenex before washing)

TUESDAY EVENING, DAY 49

7 weeks today at about this time:

Our world flipped upside down and we are slowly turning it right side up again. Bob has moved from critically severe status with life hanging in the balance to stable but guarded in just 7 weeks. He's amazing. This is a crazy ride but at least the twists and turns have smoothed out a little. Now he looks at us with this little smirk on his face and does most of the things we ask when he has the energy. The therapists apologize for asking stupid questions (like "Bob, is your name Bob?) but he continues to put up with it and respond when they ask...most of the time. As everyone says, he's on his own time schedule. One of my friends said he's just taking the scenic route back to us. We thank the good Lord for giving us time. Thanks to all of you for the continued prayers, positive thoughts and support. Each and every one of you is helping us thru this. We are truly blessed.

WEDNESDAY, MARCH 30, DAY 50

Warning - Kleenex required before reading I'm a blubbering mess. Bob said "Hi" to me today! HE SAID HI!!!!! This morning they put him in the cardiac chair (don't know why it's called that) and we went out into the solarium. It was amazing. Then speech therapist came over and he gave her a thumb's up and waved good bye. And if that wasn't enough, when we went back to the room he was mouthing words so the therapist took off the trach tube and he said "Hi" then he said, "I'm tired" and now I can't stop crying. :) GO BOB!

WEDNESDAY EVENING, DAY 50

I actually heard Bob's voice this afternoon for the first time in 7 weeks. He whispered this morning and this afternoon he actually talked. We couldn't understand the words but the sound was all Bob. I wish I could find the words to describe the feeling. Miraculous comes to mind. Bob is pooped and sleeping soundly. I hope he gets a good night's rest. He had a big day today. GO BOB!

THURSDAY, MARCH 31, DAY 51

Back up in the chair today for another round of therapy. He did really well. In my opinion, they left him up wwaaayyyy too long. He sat in the chair from 9:40 to 11:20 and then had a horrible coughing fit for about 20 minutes. Scared the pants off me. He's fine now and sound asleep. Pray the coughing is corrected. It's horrible to watch!

THURSDAY AFTERNOON, DAY 51

Bob is FINALLY sleeping. Respiratory thinks he's waking up enough now to feel the trach in his throat - eeeewww. Can you imagine? They explained it's like swallowing something wrong and coughing like crazy until it's out. Unfortunately, Bob would continue to cough like that if they didn't numb his throat. Thank you, Lord, for the medications to keep Bob comfortable and thank you, Lord, for all the progress he's made in just the past 2 weeks. GO BOB!!!

Nice meeting with all the disciplines today. I told them all what they already heard from me so there should have been no surprises. I was nice...I think...just direct. Let's see if they get it together or if the Mad Hatter has to come out and visit them :)

APRIL 2011

FRIDAY, APRIL 1, DAY 52

Direct from GO BOB central,

Bob spoke again today. His breathing is so strong he can talk around the trach. It's still emotional to hear his voice. He's not quite strong enough to form words but WOW what a miracle!!!! For all you Cubs fans, he was watching the Cubs game when he was speaking. I think he was telling them this is their year and they better just go all the way. :) He also waved to the kids and grandkids. He had the most gorgeous smile on his face while the kids were visiting. He looked truly happy. I'm still marching around here making sure Bob gets the care and attention he deserves. I must say the therapists sure have been attentive today! GO BOB!

SATURDAY, APRIL 2, DAY 53

Awesome!!! Bob is shaking his head yes and no. He mouthed words to the respiratory therapist this morning. He helped the physical therapist move his left hand, arm and leg on command. Just a minute ago, he had an itch on his eye and was trying to get his hand up there so I helped him lift that heavy ol' left arm and he wiped his eye. We stared at a few family photos this morning and he nodded when I pointed him out in the pics. Words are hard to find to describe the feeling I get seeing all this progress. He's healing himself and we're giving him the tools to do it. Hopefully by next week, we'll have even better tools for his type of injury. Please pray that Spectrum Health accepts Bob into their rehabilitation center. They are CARF (Commission on Accreditation of Rehabilitation Facilities). They also work and have experience with TBI (traumatic brain injury) patients. Borgess-Pipp provides excellent nursing care. However, the therapy here is not right for Bob's type of injury. GO BOB!

SUNDAY, APRIL 3, DAY 54

Bob was doing wonderfully this morning. He was a bit sleepy but who can blame him. It's a rainy gray Sunday in Michigan and perfect for a Sunday nap. Hopefully he rests well and gets ready for the mega therapy session I'm sure he'll have tomorrow.

We had a great visit with Spectrum Rehab this afternoon and gained a lot of knowledge, not only on Spectrum's rehabilitation program, but additional information on traumatic brain injury. We'll have to "wait and see" what happens next week. I feel like we're on a bit of a roller coaster again. Don't take your seat belt off yet! Pray we make the right decisions to help Bob get the right tools at the right time to maximize his recovery.

MONDAY, APRIL 4, DAY 55

Wow, busy day today. Speech therapy was in right at 8:00. Bob wakes up about 8:45 on his own so the 8am thing didn't work so well. Physical therapy went well. Range-of-motion exercises today. He did great but was a little sleepy. They came in right after speech. Then respiratory therapy came in to do trach care. All of this happened from about 8am to 10:30am. He dozed off for a good hour after that. This was the best I've seen him sleep since we got here.

GUESS WHAT ELSE! Spectrum accepted Bob into the program. We're moving tomorrow (Tuesday) at 10:30-ish. One thing they told us on the tour is that they work around the patient's schedule. The rehab is very patient-centric...YAY! Just one of the many great reasons this is a good choice for Bob. I spent the day packing all Bob's stuff. It's amazing how much you can accumulate in a small hospital room! Thanks to everyone for the cards, pictures, and other great stuff. I can't wait to redecorate in the new digs at Spectrum. LOOK OUT 'CAUSE HERE COMES BOB!!! GO BOB! :)

TUESDAY, APRIL 5, DAY 56

What a super day. Bob had a great trip to Spectrum Health. He was very alert this afternoon and even "talked" for the new speech therapist. Perfect timing! I was with the social worker going over Bob's info so I missed it but he "talks" to me a lot so I'm over it. I just hate to miss anything. I can tell you it's a relief to be in a program that specializes in Bob's type of injury. We'll "wait and see" how he does and pray for the right tools at the right time to ensure the best possible recovery. It was 8 weeks ago today at about this time Bob had his horrible accident. Phase 1 involved the critical care unit at Borgess and praying for survival. Phase 2 involved the long term acute care tools at Borgess-Pipp and praying that

Bob would emerge from his coma while recovering from his other medical issues. Phase 3 brings us to Spectrum Health because Bob has the ability to interact with his environment and he is medically stable. We pray for guidance, patience and understanding during the long hard road ahead for Bob. We are very thankful to have the opportunity to provide a recovery plan. Continued prayers and support will move us through this. Thank you everyone! GO BOB!

WEDNESDAY, APRIL 6, DAY 57

Bob's new room doesn't have a white board with the day and date. I'm going to be lost. I'm still stuck in February. Speech, occupation and physical therapy came in this morning and all went well. They put my mind at ease...FINALLY! They were very calm, quiet and kept the stimulus to a minimum while they sat Bob up on the side of the bed. He did beautifully! He took a little nap and then was awake this afternoon for awhile, mouthed words and smiled at everyone who came in the door. Obviously, these people know what they're doing. The goal is to get him comfortable in a chair for 2 hours, which they will build up to instead of just putting him the stupid chair for 2 hours!

I'm still trying to figure out the Spectrum wi-fi network. I can connect but it won't let me post for some reason. I'll have to figure that out in the next few days so the updates might be a little later than usual. Thank you everyone for your continued support. Again, it's an absolute miracle we've gotten this far and have been given this incredible opportunity for Bob to become the best Bob he can be. GO BOB!

THURSDAY, APRIL 7, DAY 58

Bob is amazing and so is his therapy team! Speech therapy this morning was very encouraging. They plan to do speech twice a day starting next week. She was very positive about what she saw with Bob, which made me all excited. He also sat in the chair this morning for 1-1/2 hours with no problems. Low lighting in the room and quiet talking with just me and he did beautifully. Low stimulation is the key. This afternoon he had range-of-motion and he was able to respond to commands on his left side. This is so exciting! The therapists talk quietly and keep the lights low. They are so encouraging and positive with Bob it's great to see. Here's a funny little tid bit - the therapist asked him to push back with his right leg and he tried and tried. Pretty soon, up comes the left hand and it looked like he was trying to push his right leg down! The therapist didn't say HOW to make the leg push back. Ha! That's so Bob :) Guess what else? They asked me to bring in a white board for his room so we can put the day and date on it. I almost laughed out loud. Seeing as how I told Bob it was Tuesday when it was really Wednesday, I think I'm the one that needs the white board. GO BOB!

FRIDAY, APRIL 8, DAY 59

Wonderful day again today. I told Bob I was going to have lunch with some friends and he said, "OK." He actually said, "OK"!!!!! He still has that stupid trach, too. Only 5 more days with the neck brace (we hope) and then we can start to get rid of that trach. I can't even imagine the day when we can start talking together again. It will be out-of-this-world spectacular! He was up in the chair for 2 hours this morning and they're going to get him up tonight, too. It was very difficult to leave knowing that sometime tonight they are going to put him in his chair but I acknowledge that I can't be there 24/7 and he's in a great place. I know they'll take good care of him. His physical/occupational therapy is going really well. Unfortunately, he continues to sleep for the speech therapist. She's going to try to stop by when he's in his chair so he's awake and ready to "talk." You guys are amazing, too. I write about a white board and - viola - we had a white board by 9am this morning. My neighbors think I'm too skinny so they brought me out to a lunch buffet and then bought a pizza for me to take home. I already ate half the pizza, too! Thanks to everyone for your continued support. Bob is really working hard now and will need lots of support, positive reinforcement, and encouragement. GO BOB!

SATURDAY, APRIL 9, DAY 60

C-collar removal = 4 days and counting. Actually, Weds is the X-RAY to make sure the C-collar can come off. We are praying for good tests results! Once the C-collar is off we can start to take the steps to get rid of that stupid trach!

Bob is starting to answer yes and no questions and actually shaking his head no. He's really good at yes if he needs something but I just figured if he didn't do anything, then the answer was no. Now he can do both yes AND no. YAY! Today the aide asked how he was doing and he said "good." He actually said that clear as day! In the past 2 days, he's clearly said "ok" and "good." He also grabbed on to the strings on my sweatshirt and pulled them tight and, of course, smiled. It must have felt good to be able to coordinate all the movements and actually grab on to the strings. AMAZING! The things our bodies just do without thought take every ounce of energy and coordination for Bob. I can't even imagine the strength it takes to talk over his trach. GO BOB!

SUNDAY, APRIL 10, DAY 61

Holy Schnykees what a great day! Let me explain the most amazing thing I've seen in nearly 9 weeks and see if I can do it justice. Bob was sitting in his chair this morning so I took the opportunity to straighten up his hair. I showed Bob the comb and asked if I could comb his hair. He nodded so I went ahead (nodding is still a relatively new accomplishment and is a great thing all by itself!). When I was done, I showed him the comb again. He reached up with his left hand, took the comb and proceeded to try and get his left arm up so he could comb his own hair. THIS IS SO AMAZ-ING! His brain recognized a comb AND knew what to do with it AND told his left hand to grasp the comb AND told his left hand to comb his hair! He then proceeded to look at me with a little grin on his face as if to say, "Are you going to cry again? It's just a comb." And yes I had tears in my eyes again. If Bob's motivation is to see if he can get me to cry, then I'm all for it. GO BOB!

MONDAY, APRIL 11, DAY 62

C-collar removal = 2 days and counting. I've told everyone that I've put a lot of eggs in the Wednesday basket so we PRAY that the collar truly can come off!!!

We were able to take Bob out of his room and sit by some big windows that overlook the nice outdoors. It was wonderful to see how well he did on his travels. Anytime somebody walked by, he had to watch what they were doing...just like at home. At one point he was so comfortable, he took a little snooze. It's hard to describe how it feels to see him in his own chair that fits him so well. Safe and secure come to mind. My driving skills, however, leave a bit to be desired. Yesterday the nurse told Bob that my driving skills needed a bit of improvement before she would let me leave the room (I ran his foot rests into the bed...twice!). We laughed and Bob had a big grin on his face so we decided to just sit in his room and look out the window. Today Dad helped with the IV pole while I navigated Bob thru the hallways. I'm happy to report that we didn't take out any little old ladies and we only had trouble dodging the cleaning cart. Otherwise all went well. He also went to the low-stim gym. It's this really quiet low-lit room that is perfect for Bob. We worked his legs and he did magnificent! His left side is getting so strong he can move it all over mostly on command sometimes just because he wants to. And of course, anytime someone came in or out, he had to check 'em out so he was just a little distracted but over all a great workout.

Everyday Bob progresses and it's truly a miracle to watch. I'm thankful I can be a part of this miracle. GO BOB!

TUESDAY, APRIL 12, DAY 63

C-Collar Removal = less than 24 hours...we PRAY!!!

GO BOB Central here again - I witnessed truly spectacular events today! I just hope I can convey the magnitude of these events. This morning Bob worked with the speech therapist. She will hold up objects and tell Bob to reach for them. He followed her every word AND he picked up the fork and brought it to his lips AND he picked up the pen and was holding it like he wanted to write. Therapist got out a piece of paper and he tried to write his name!!!! DO YOU GET THE MAGNITUDE OF THIS?!!! Bob picks out objects, picks them up and then can use them appropriately. THAT'S HUGE!!!!! He also went to the low-stim gym again. They sat him on the edge of a raised mat and worked on his core muscles. He was able to pull himself forward and push himself back. The first time he pulled forward, he grabbed the therapist's hand for help. They were so excited that he problem-solved his way to moving that they cut him some slack. Both therapists started laughing, Bob had a HUGE grin on his face and I was laughing thru my tears! :) Lots of happy tears today! GO BOB!

WEDNESDAY, APRIL 13, DAY 64

WOO HOO! BOB'S BRACE FREE! C-Collar and turtle shell back brace are no more! Neck's fine. Back's healing. GO BOB! He tolerated the one-hour drive to Kalamazoo and back just fine. I got to ride along in the ambulance up front. Of course, I wanted to turn on all the lights and sirens but they wouldn't let me. They're so serious...geez☺ As soon as we had him all settled back in his room, he was sound asleep. He looks so peaceful and comfortable without that brace. IT'S WONDERFUL! I'm sure he'll sleep well tonight. Back up and at 'em tomorrow for therapy. I fully expect him to be sleepy tomorrow but we'll see. He is amazing all of us with his strength and energy! GO BOB!

Bob will be slowly weaned (I have no idea how to spell that) off the trach. As from day 1, he's on his own schedule, but here are the steps:

> 1. Downsize the inner canula, which will allow a speaking valve to go on. 2. Put on a speaking valve, which allows air to go in but he will have to exhale thru his mouth and nose. This will allow air over his vocal cords. We'll need to work on the muscles that haven't been used in a long time so speaking will be hard at first. 3. Cap the trach altogether so he has to breathe in and out thru his mouth and nose. 4. Once he tolerates having it capped, the whole thing will be removed! YAY!

THURSDAY, APRIL 14, DAY 65

Bob was sleepy today so we tried to take it easy on him. We were able to take a little tour around the hallways and Bob did just fine. I think he likes being out of the room so he can people watch. I'm also happy to report I only hit the wall once with the footrests. Thank goodness it was when we were parking to look out the windows. You should see all the stuff we have to navigate - narrow doorways, empty wheel chairs, cleaning carts, people. We've gotten pretty good at it though. We also went to the gym again. Bob worked on his core muscles and did AWESOME! He went from side to side today and did great. They also made him pull forward and push back again. He's amazingly strong (and good looking but maybe that's TMI). It's GREAT to see him move without any braces! I gotta believe it feels better to move around freely. He holds his head up just fine with a little bit of a lean to the left but therapy will take care of that. Looking forward to what tomorrow brings!

Thank you to all my work buddies for the great poster and all your inspirational messages! It says GO BOB with an exclamation point in the middle of the O in the GO. It's perfect! We love it! GO BOB!

FRIDAY, APRIL 15, DAY 66

Bob did really well today. The speech therapist had playing cards out and he was able to identify them correctly and take them from her. All those hours in front of the computer playing Texas Hold 'Em finally paid off! And, if that weren't cool enough, in the gym today they put him on a tilt-table and "stood" him up. He did great! His blood pressure was stable and he tolerated it just fine. It was amazing to see him "standing" for the first time in nearly 10 weeks.

The therapists wore him out today with range-of-motion exercises and the tilt-table experience. We asked for some Tylenol about 4:00 but around 5:00 he was still sore so he's going to get the really good stuff in just a few minutes. Thank goodness! I'll have to pay attention and help manage his pain better. We should have asked for the Vicadin at 4 instead of the Tylenol. Lesson learned.

We also took our morning tour around the building and Bob was very content watching the maintenance guys change light bulbs down one of the hallways. I bet we sat there for nearly 45 minutes watching those guys. Bob didn't fidget or get anxious or anything. I think it made him feel good to see normal work stuff instead of hospital-type stuff. AND, I didn't run into anything today....I'm sure Bob thanks me for that. Another awesome day in Bob's recovery! GO BOB!

SATURDAY, APRIL 16, DAY 67

Bob sat in his chair for a while this morning so we took a tour around the building. His brothers and sister-in-law were able to visit and stroll along with us. He wears his sun glasses when we tour because 1) bright lights are hard on anybody's eyes but especially survivors of a brain injury, 2) he wore sun glasses all the time before the accident and 3) he just looks cool! When Bob was getting ready to lay down I asked if he wanted to keep his sun glasses on and he reached up, took them off and handed them to me. I guess that would be a no :) VERY COOL! Bob is getting so strong and starting to move so much that he can discom-"bob"-ulate himself around in his bed. He was lying on the side rail with his head hanging over the side today. NOT COOL! So, now we have to stay one step ahead of his abilities. He has bumpers around his bed now that will keep him safe. He was all snug as a bug when I left tonight. Thank goodness! He also does a lot of exploring with his left hand so he has to wear a mitt that keeps his fingers from grabbing things they shouldn't (like his trach and his feeding tube!). I'm just thankful they have nice "restraints" that allow him the freedom of motion he's working so hard to get back and that also keep him safe. It is wonderful and shocking and crazy and awesome that he's moving so much we have to be worried. GO BOB!

SUNDAY, APRIL 17, DAY 68

Wow...Palm Sunday already? Time is just weird right now.

Bob had a pretty quiet Sunday. We went for our morning walk-about with great success. I avoided all the obstacles and Bob just enjoyed the ride. We also worked on some object identification so he's ready for the speech therapist tomorrow. I'm happy to report he knows all the tools...hammer, screwdriver, tape measure. I have to remind him that I know these seem like simple questions but it's important to show he knows so he can move on to the next level. After I explain this, it's like a switch comes on and he's alert and aware. IT'S MAGNIFICENT...HE'S MAGNIFICENT!

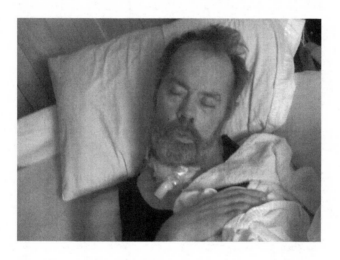

Bonus for the day - respiratory therapist stopped by to let Bob know that his trach will be down-sized on Tuesday and she's going to skip the whole speaking valve thing and go right to a cap...AWESOME! That means he will potentially be able to speak depending on how much effort it takes. TOTALLY AWESOME! It also means that once he's adjusted to the cap on the trach and does well with it, the whole trach will come out.

TOTALLY AWESOME TO THE MAX! :)

I'm being well taken care of too. Thank you to my great neighbors who made a wonderful meal. My favorite... grilled chicken with Quinoa, green beans and salad. Bonus for me - gluten free brownies, my FAVORITE! I'll try not to eat the whole batch tonight. My belly will thank me. :)

MONDAY, APRIL 18, DAY 69

Bob had a great day today with the speech therapist. He's doing so well we're going to try a communication board. I'm not sure what kind or what type but I'm sure I'll know soon enough. It will be a new gadget for Bob to try and he loves gadgets.

We also went to the gym today. He had a mirror in front of him so he could tell when he was sitting up straight. That was the first time he saw himself and he didn't seem to mind the big bushy beard and long curly locks he has goin' on. Although it could be he was just concentrating on his workout and not really his looks.

Big day tomorrow! Pray for a safe and successful downsizing of the trach. I'm always a little nervous about these things even though I know he'll do just fine. In fact, it's way over due. He's ready for sure! GO BOB!

TUESDAY, APRIL 19, DAY 70

WOO HOO!

Trach capped and Bob spoke!!!!!! His voice is a whisper but it's his! His first word was "door." The therapist said this was a long shot but she explained she was going to start a sentence and ask Bob to finish it. She said, "Bob, we can open a..." Then she said, "da..." and Bob said, "door"! UN-FLIP-PIN-BELIEVABLE! Then she asked his last name and he said, "Kamps" with out any prompting. He works really hard and has to concentrate to get out the words. He really uses a lot of energy to verbalize and vocalize. After he spoke, I asked if he heard his voice and he nodded. IT WAS ABSOLUTE-LY AMAZING! And that's not all. I, of course, had tears in my eyes and told him it was so wonderful to hear his voice I couldn't help it. Do you know what he did? He rolled his eyes at me! HA! I laughed through my tears, blew my nose, and he just grinned at me. That is so Bob. :)

WEDNESDAY, APRIL 20, DAY 71

Bob's whisper is still wonderful! Because Bob was intubat-ed for 16 days and he's not yet drinking water, his vocal cords are dry and have scar tissue (gross)...not to mention he had a dental pick in his throat!!!! He's working really hard to whisper words and communicate. He's never been a chatty Cathy so I know he's saving his energy to say those things that are important. He did send out a string of words to the therapists today but we didn't quite catch what he said. They were stretching his right side, which is not com-fortable for him AT ALL. I'm pretty sure there were a few choice words in that string!

THURSDAY, APRIL 21, DAY 72

Little bit of a tough day today. Bob's right side is very uncom-fortable and we're having some difficulty managing the pain. We started with Vicadin at 8:30 then again at 1:30 and again at 5:00. He's also struggling to speak more and more, which takes so much energy and concentration. We didn't take our morning stroll because Bob was not comfortable at all. Af-ter speech therapy he was a little riled up and couldn't seem to get relaxed. He really works hard to speak and I think it might be a little frustrating that the words take so much ef-fort. He also had little bites of applesauce to test his swallow-ing ability. It's been more than 10 weeks since he's had food in his mouth and I'm ECSTATIC to report he did just fine!!!!

This afternoon we were able to take a little tour thru the halls and we ran into the recreational therapist. As usual, Bob had his sunglasses on and she asked if the lights were bothering his eyes. He said, and I quote, "not too bad." WOW! I think the excitement of hearing him answer a question will never go away! :) GO BOB!

FRIDAY, APRIL 22, DAY 73

GOOD FRIDAY MIRACLES ENCLOSED!!!!

TRACH IS GONE!!!!! WOO HOO!!!! It took literally 5 seconds. No coughing, no pain, no problems. Bob looks more comfortable already. ALL SET WITH SWALLOWING! Speech therapist did a blue dye test for swallowing and Bob passed with flying colors. Next week Bob may try other things besides applesauce! STANDING ON HIS OWN 2 FEET! After physical therapy, they transfer Bob back to his chair from the mat. Today they had him stand for a second and he helped. He did so well they're going to try standing on Monday! SPEAKING MORE AND MORE! Ang and Joel stopped by to visit and Ang brought the grand kids. When they came in, Bob said, "holy cow." Then he said (with just a little bit of help), "Hi Holly" and "Hi Laura."

I know I'm overusing the word "miracle" but what Bob is able to accomplish every day is truly miraculous.

One more thing, when Bob is trying really hard to get the words out, he reaches up and pulls my ear down to his mouth so I can better hear his voice. My ears hurt. :) GO BOB!

SATURDAY, APRIL 23, DAY 73

Bob had a nice relaxing day. Up in the chair this morning and again this evening and a nice, long Saturday afternoon nap. His brother Mike came to visit and when Mike came around the corner, I said, "Your brother's here." Bob turned his head, looked at Mike and said "Michael." I wish I could share the tone he used. Imagine you pass someone in a hallway, do one head nod, and then say their full name. That's what it sounded like. It was classic Bob! HA! ☺ GO BOB!

SUNDAY, APRIL 24, DAY 74

What a great day. Bob was able to enjoy the great outdoors today. It was in the low 60s here and kinda sunny. Definitely warm enough for Bob so outside we went. It was great! He looked very relaxed in his chair and we were able to keep the chair on the sidewalk - woo hoo! When we came back in, he told his brother Mike, and I quote, "this place is boring." I'll remind him tomorrow after therapy that he thought this place was boring. Later this evening, he told his other brother Bruce, wife Lori and nieces Brianna and Lyndsie, "this place is stupid, stupid, stupid"! HA! All good signs. Good thing they have alarms on the doors because next thing you know, Bob will be making a break for it. Our new cheer might have to be "STAY BOB" until he's actually safe enough to "GO"! STAY-GO BOB!

MONDAY, APRIL 25, DAY 75

BOB IS AMAZING!!! He had chocolate pudding today to make sure he's swallowing efficiently. He's doing so well he most likely won't need a video swallow test (which has to be done at the hospital, so no trip to the hospital) and he'll be eating soft foods soon - woo hoo! The other good news - he's a lefty and his left side is fine so using utensils is a non-issue! After 30 minutes of speech therapy and 30 minutes of physical therapy, I asked Bob if he was bored today. He shook his head no. I think being bored was a brief experience. Maybe this weekend, I'll turn on the Rolling Stones and dance around with my tongue hanging out. That should be entertaining...at least for the cleaning people :)

I LOVE MY NEIGHBORS!

Thanks to my wonderful neighbors for the great Easter dinner. There was enough for two nights (and probably three but I was hungry!) Also, our boat escaped from the dock and was roaming aimlessly around the lake. Thanks to more wonderful neighbors for returning it safely back to its home at the dock. Another amazing, awesome, glorious, super fantastic day in Bob's recovery! GO BOB!

TUESDAY, APRIL 26, DAY 76

Bob had a rather melancholy day today. He mentioned something about a car and having an accident. I believe he's trying to put the pieces together to figure out why he is where he is and what happened.

He did excellent during therapy today. He stood up for about 3 minutes twice. It was amazing! I forgot how tall he is. Therapist asked how tall he is and he said, "six two." Well, there ya go. I wasn't sure and now I know. :) During speech therapy, he was eating cottage cheese and the speech therapist told him to say "AH" as long as he could so she could make sure he's swallowing correctly. He looked at me and then at her and said in his strong voice, "that's just strange" and shook his head no. HA! Therapist said, "that's good enough for me" and we all laughed. Little bits of Bob's personality are starting to emerge! GO BOB! Brother Jack arrived from Denver today. YAY! We have 2 cats and Jack has a dog. So far, they've avoided each other but it's only been a few hours. I'll let you know who wins...(my money is on the kitties).

WEDNESDAY, APRIL 27, DAY 77

Another great day for Bob. Cherry cobbler and cranberry juice for a snack during speech therapy. The truly amazing part is not one drop of cobbler or juice landed on his WHITE t-shirt. How many of US are coordinated enough to do that? :)

The progress Bob has made in just the past week is amazing. He's strong enough and balanced enough to sit up straight pretty much on his own. Today was just the second day with standing and he's already much straighter and he stood much longer. Just last week he didn't have enough strength to pull himself forward while sitting. Now...piece a cake (or should I say cobbler)!

He talks all the time now too. He's still whispering so we're trying to get him to use his strong voice. The more he uses his vocal cords, the easier it will get. Eating and swallowing will help with the voice as well. Not to worry though. I'll keep talking for the both of us :) GO BOB!

THURSDAY, APRIL 28, DAY 78

Bob had a peanut butter and jelly sandwich today - PB and grape jelly on whole wheat bread! Unbelievable! So cool! He will start going to lunch on Monday and eat in the low-stim dining room (low lights, just a few people, and quiet-quiet-quiet).

Bob now has a brace for his right wrist and a ratchet brace for his right elbow. When they put the brace on the elbow he said, "TOO TIGHT" so they loosened it, thank goodness.

With a name like "ratchet", I can only imagine what it feels like! I'm so glad he is starting to communicate and can get the words out when it's important. He was also fitted for a foot brace to help keep his right foot straight and flat. He's starting to move his right side more and more - all of which will help with the stiffness. The braces are to prevent permanent contraction of the muscles so the stronger he gets, the less need for braces.

We're also working on getting a new chair. Let's hope it's easier to steer so I'm less of a menace in the hallways! GO BOB!

FRIDAY, APRIL 29, DAY 79

Bob is amazing. He is working so hard! Today during range-of-motion on his right side, it was really tight. He was in quite a bit of discomfort but took a few deep breaths and kept going. It really helps that the therapist will count down so he knows how long he has to go. He's the model patient and they all wish every patient was as easy to work with as Bob. Even the nurses have said he's so cooperative they love working with him.

We keep the room really calm-low lights, quiet and window open for a cool breeze. He also has a fan because he's just a hot guy! After pouring every ounce of energy into his workouts, Bob needs lots of rest and he's never liked noise so I think his room suits him well. The staff will stop by during the day just to say hi but I think they really just want to hide out in the quiet cool room.

More standing today and Bob stood up on his own!

He's getting so strong it's wonderful to see. Therapist asked how it felt and Bob said, "like it used too." YAY!

Cat/Dog update - cats rule! GO BOB!

MAY 2011

SUNDAY, MAY 1, DAY 81

HAPPY 18TH ANNIVERSARY BOB! We celebrated our anniversary by touring the hallways and enjoying the great outdoors today. Bob was up and in his chair from 1 to 4 this afternoon and wanted to keep moving. I believe we toured about 300 miles around the same hallways and outdoor walkways for 3 hours. If you need to know where anything is at Spectrum Health and Rehabilitation Center, we gotchya covered. Linen closets, education room, custodial services, facility manager, dining rooms, snack shop, flowers in bloom and flowers yet to bloom, pond, gazebo, back parking lot - we saw it all and most of it more than once. What a work out. My feet hurt and Bob was sound asleep when I left. He didn't sleep well last night so the plan was to keep him up today so he would sleep tonight. Hopefully, our plan worked and he sleeps well to get ready for tomorrow.

Ang, Joel and Ang's husband Bob are the best kids ever. They took me out for dinner last night to celebrate our anniversary and gave me a gift certificate for a massage. You guys are wonderful and are handling this whole incredible twist of fate remarkably well. I'm so glad you are there for your dad and me. Your support means a lot to both of us. Big day tomorrow for Bob. Lunch in the dining room. Cool! Looking forward to letting you all know what's on the menu. GO BOB!

MONDAY, MAY 2, DAY 82

Wonderful, wonderful, wonderful day! Speech therapist asked Bob to finish sentences today and he did great! She asked him to finish the following, "Wash your..." and Bob said "work clothes." He had a tough time with "tie your..." because the "sh" sound is hard but when she said "shoes" he said "yes." YAY! Then right after that we went to the gym and Bob stood up on the standing frame. He got half way up and pulled himself up the rest of the way. It was fantastic to watch. He stood up for nearly 10 minutes! Half way thru the therapists realized he wasn't even using the harness that holds him upright because he was already upright when it was time for the harness. YAY! Fifteen minute break and then off we went to the dining room for lunch. BBQ Chicken, baked potato, corn, drinks and coffee. Again, he did fantastic! He ate about half the meal and said, "I think I'm done." That is a classic Bob statement. He would say that after every big meal. Then he said yes to some milk so as I'm getting the lid off, he reaches out and in a flash grabbed the lemon drink and pretty much chugged it down. I freaked out because I was thinking, "that's too much, that's too much!" but speech therapist was fine with it and had a big smile on her face so I guess he was fine!

YAY! GO BOB!

TUESDAY, MAY 3, DAY 83

3 months ago today marked the beginning of a new life for Bob. At the time, who knew if survival was part of the plan. Now here he is on the road to recovery. 5 weeks in the Neuro-Critical Unit (NCU)- Feb 8 to March 15 - three weeks at the LTACH - March 15 to April 5 - and 4 weeks in rehab - April 5 to May 3. WOW! He's come along way in just 12 weeks!

We are incredibly fortunate that Bob is doing so well. He's getting stronger every day. His speech is improving every day. He's working hard every day. It truly is a miracle. Your continued prayers, support and well wishes are getting us through this. THANK YOU! GO BOB!

BTW - tuna noodle casserole, green beans, whole-wheat roll and coffee for lunch. AWESOME! ☺

WEDNESDAY, MAY 4, DAY 84

Bob has a new chair because he doesn't need all the gadgets to help keep him sitting up right! YAY! It's your basic wheel chair but with a taller back that reclines. Very nice. It even has a nice pillow for his head. There's a Velcro lap belt that keeps him safe so we'll see how long that lasts. It has an alarm so if he pulls it off, we'll know and yes, he's figured out how to pull it off. Lots of redirection and looking for more interesting things to fiddle with today. He's getting to be a handful and it's the most wonderful thing EVER! Words cannot describe how elated I am that he's becoming more and more active. SAFETY FIRST! I'm thinking about wrapping him in bubble wrap and making him wear a motorcycle helmet all the time now. Today at lunch I almost lost a finger! The tray had barely reached the table and Bob grabbed the fork, flipped the lid off the plate and went to town on the mashed potatoes and gravy. Either he has his appetite back or he knows there's a 2-hour nap waiting for him after lunch. I'm betting on the nap. As soon as he was lying down, he was fast asleep. Stop and think for a moment how much energy, coordination and planning goes into the simple act of eating. Bob can put all of those things together and eat his own meal. Marvelous! Glorious, wonderful, magnificent, spectacular Bob! GO BOB!

THURSDAY, MAY 5, DAY 85

Another great day for Bob. He's eating so well at lunch he's going to start eating three meals a day in the dining room on Monday! So Cool! He also did really well during therapy and I was able to give him a back rub while he was lying on his stomach. I've been promising that for a long time and I was finally able to deliver. He's an outstanding spectacular man and it shows every day in his attitude, his hard work and his bright gorgeous smile. GO BOB!

FRIDAY, MAY 6, DAY 86

Wow...busy, busy, busy. 9:30 up and at 'em. 10-10:30 laying on his stomach in the gym, 10:30-11 speech therapy (and he aced everything!!!!), 11-11:30 back to the gym for stretching the right arm (very painful but he worked through it), 11:30 to 12 stretching his trunk muscles (so strong he can reach down and touch his ankle!), 12-12:30 lunch (fish, rice, carrots, milk and coffee) and finally a well earned 2 hour nap. From 2:30 to 3, range of motion on his right leg. Thankfully, the 2:30 session is done in his room while he's lying down. He was able to get a little nap in until nearly 5 and then back up until 7. Brother Bruce and Lori took him outside for a nice evening tour of the grounds.

Bob worked so hard this week he definitely earned a nice calm relaxing weekend. Hopefully he doesn't get too bored and will sleep well. Next week we start three meals in the dining room. Up and at 'em around 7:30! Oy...I already need a nap. :) GO BOB!

SATURDAY, MAY 7, DAY 87

I'm going to need new walking shoes! Bob is so active we have to keep moving or he tries to get up out of his chair. I asked him what he was doing and he said, "I need to stand up." We also have to stay out of the room or he takes off his safety alarm and tries to get into bed. He was very, very, very fidgety during lunch and I'm sure I didn't help. He kept sliding down in his chair and I kept trying to pull him back up. After about half his meal he said, and I quote, "I'm sick of this." I asked if he was sick of lunch and he said, "No, I'm sick of this whole thing." Then he said he was sick to his stomach so I took that as a cue to leave the dining room. Even low stimulus is still too much during meals. We'll have to come up with a better plan tomorrow.

About 3:30 I turned on golf and all seemed right with the world. Calm, relaxed and just hangin' out watching golf. Now that's a normal weekend activity for the Kamps! :) GO BOB!

SUNDAY, MAY 8, DAY 88

Much more relaxed day today for Bob. We spent the morning touring the grounds outside. Gorgeous day today in Michigan. Lunch went extremely well and Bob ate the whole thing...YAY! We were one of the first to the dining room so we sat at a table that faced the wall. It was just me and Bob. Quiet, no distractions and he could concentrate on eating. He is a rather speedy eater. I have to remind him that the muscles are getting stronger so it's important to chew and swallow before the next bite. He seems to be fine with that and will set his fork down and relax between bites. We should all probably do that anyway. :) GO BOB!

MONDAY, MAY 9, DAY 89

It was great to hear Bob's voice today!!!! During speech therapy, he has to use his strong voice to answer questions. He will answer correctly but if he doesn't say it loud enough, he has to say it again. It takes a lot of effort but it's getting easier for him. It's so wonderful to hear!!!

He also walked on his knees today...SO COOL! He was on the mat and upright on his knees. Just like walking except on his knees instead of his feet. He is getting so strong it's AMAZING! And here's the best part. He moved his RIGHT leg! The therapist had his leg bent at the knee and told him to kick it up. He did it all on his own 4 of the 5 times. So now we know the right leg works too!

This was another spectacular day for Bob. He's making great progress and working really, really hard all day. He earns every minute of every rest period during the day and seems to be sleeping better at night. He's amazing and just keeps getting more amazing every day! GO BOB!

TUESDAY, MAY 10, DAY 90

What a busy day! Bob only had about 45 minutes of rest this morning. His schedule was all messed up. We had therapists coming and going all morning so I finally put a stop to it. Bob has to have rest! The hairs on the back of my neck were standing up. All I kept thinking about was the other place that did the same thing. The good thing is they listened to me so we'll see if it's any better tomorrow. He did have about 2-1/2 hours of sleep this afternoon and we literally had to wake him up for dinner. Poor guy. He was exhausted. I'm glad there are so many things we need to fit into the day because he's getting so active. What a great problem to have to solve. We just have to make sure we solve with Bob's best interest in mind. If you were wondering about Bob's sense of humor, I asked him to say my name in his strong voice today so he said, "Cyndi Kamps." It was the most beautiful thing I've ever heard! After he said it, he followed it with, "you don't know your own name?" with this half a smirk on his face. HA! The aide told him she'd be back in about an hour to get him up and he said, "I'll be waiting for ya." Yesterday, the speech therapist said, "see ya later" and he said, "alligator." What a ham! :) GO BOB!

THURSDAY, MAY 12, DAY 92

Bob had Botox today in his right arm so now he has younger looking muscles :) Actually, the Botox will weaken the muscle so it stops contracting and causing so much pain. Speaking of pain, the shots in his lower arm were VERY PAINFUL. He had a rough morning. We finally made it back to his room and he took a 2-hour nap. Yikes, it's hard to see your best friend and better half in so much pain but as always, he powered through it. The doc called him a rock star for handling it so well. In 7 to 14 days we should see the full affects of how well the Botox will work. Praying for a successful procedure so he can regain use of his right arm. It was 100 million degrees at Spectrum today. Apparently there is some state rule about turning the heat off and the air on. I'm finding there are a ton of stupid rules and people just don't think. DUH! If it's 87 out, turn the frickin' air on! It was actually cooler outside because there was a breeze. Thank goodness Bob has a fan in his room (other than me...HA). One more day of therapy and then two well deserved days of rest. GO BOB!

MONDAY, MAY 16, DAY 96

Bob is awesome! Everyone is very excited about his progress. He's very, very, very thin and I'm very concerned BUT his appetite is fantastic and he gained 3 pounds over the weekend. Hopefully the pounds stay on.

Right now he has what they call nectar-thick liquids to make sure he can control the swallow. Today he tried normal milk and did just fine. Tomorrow at lunch he'll have all regular liquids. Very exciting! I'll be able to get him glasses of water throughout the day instead of ordering them from the kitchen. Also, after trying the milk, the speech therapist asked Bob if she could hear his voice to make sure the milk went down the right hatch. She said, "Bob, can I hear your voice?" and he said in his loud strong deep voice, "Why yes you can." I LOVE IT! There were four of us at the table and we all chuckled. :)

I've made a vow to myself to take the afternoons off. Bob sleeps from 2:30 until 5 when it's time to get up for dinner. I'm going to force myself to leave for at least an hour. The last few days I've been less than a stellar caregiver. Time to regroup. I got stuck in the mire and forgot about the future. Ooops. Good thing Spectrum provides support for the caregivers too and I'm smart enough to know when I need it. My brother threatened to punch me if I didn't start doing something for myself once in awhile. Dog/Cat Update - all is well. Now tolerating each other in the same room. GO BOB!

WEDNESDAY, MAY 18, DAY 98

BOB WALKED TODAY!!!!!!! I cried for 30 minutes!

It was UNBELIEVABLE! They used what's called an Eva walker. Bob rested his forearms on the walker and the therapists helped him place his feet. He brought his left foot forward and they would move his right. He walked about 20 feet and then rested for a minute and walked another 20 feet to his chair. What made me so emotional was when he sat down in his chair. He said out loud in his beautiful strong, low voice, "I WALKED"!

HUGE GYNOURMOUS MILE STONE FOR BOB! GO BOB!

THURSDAY, MAY 19, DAY 99

Bob had a haircut and a beard trim today and HOLY CRAP he looks just like Bob again! Wow! Who knew a little beauty treatment could make such a difference. He now has his summer cut. :) We finally got the wheel chair fixed today. They couldn't raise it so they put a big cushion on the seat and now he sits up tall and proud. He looks so much more comfortable and he was able to sit for 2 hours tonight with no problems. We sat in his room, ate dinner and watched the news... just like at home (minus the wheel chair, hospital disinfectant smell and institutional food...other than that, just like at home). He's having an amazing week. Second week eating 3 squares a day and he's on his way! Crazy what food will do. And, by the way, HE WALKED YESTERDAY and he'll be doing more walking tomorrow! WOO HOO! GO BOB!

FRIDAY, MAY 20, DAY 100

Superman Bob walked down the hallway today. The more he walked the better the rhythm, which made his right leg move even more than on Wednesday. Absolutely phenomenal! He is amazing! Tonight I asked him if anything hurt and he said "everything" so he got some more good drugs. He's working so hard!!!! Lots of rest and relaxation this weekend so he can get ready for next week and more therapy. We met a young man who had a similar injury in August of 2010. He came back to visit. It was wonderful to see how well he's doing. He gave Bob a little pep talk and reminded him why he's working so hard and Bob smiled and said, "yep." So nice to see Bob interacting more and more. Here's a good one. I was helping Bob get situated in the bed and every single time I adjusted the bed, I hit the wrong button. He ends up going up and down like a yo-yo until I find the right button. He finally asked me if it was all the way down and then he said, "why does it do that?" I had to explain to him that his dorky wife keeps hitting the wrong buttons. Hopefully I don't end up making him into a taco all sandwiched in his bed, poor guy :)

MONDAY, MAY 23, DAY 103

Bob was in quite a bit of pain today. Fortunately good drugs and understanding staff helped him through it. The therapists were able to work around his schedule today and had therapy a little bit later than usual. Being the super hero that he is, he walked down the hallway again. He's a rock star! Starting tomorrow at lunch, he'll try a general diet. If all goes well, he can eat anything he wants and start picking his own menu. YAY! His feeding tube will remain until he gains some weight. He's lost 40 pounds! Praying for pain free days for Bob! GO BOB!

FRIDAY, MAY 27, DAY 107

Our home internet isn't workin right. Our provider is waiting for a part from China to get it fixed so updates will be delayed. Bob's doing super fantastic. He starts a general diet today and has normal liquids again so he can eat and drink whatever he wants. He even gets to pick out his own meals. Last night we went thru the menu for today and Bob picked out really good stuff. I was surprised when he picked baked Pollock over beef casserole but hey, I'm all for healthy eating :)

We're planning an afternoon out and are trying to think of something to do. I suggested a pizza party or a picnic in a park. Someone else suggested Meijer gardens. Anyone else have any ideas? I'm so excited for Bob to have an afternoon off and a break in his schedule!!! WOO HOO! GO BOB!

SATURDAY, MAY 28, DAY 108

Bob walked 272 feet yesterday! Twice as far as on Thursday. He was still breathing really hard but he just kept right on going. SO COOL! I still cry every time. I'm going to have to work on that.

We also play the card game War now. It's the easiest to play because he doesn't have to hold any cards. We just make a pile on the table. So far, it's 3 to 1 in favor of Bob. Today will be a day of rest, relaxation, eating and visiting. Hope all goes well for Bob. Sometimes the weekends are hard because he doesn't have anything structured. Praying for a pain-free unboring weekend.

SUNDAY, MAY 29, DAY 109

Bob didn't sleep very well Saturday night so today was a make up day. He slept pretty much all day. We had nasty thunderstorms this afternoon - a perfect day for a Sunday afternoon nap. I put in a movie and we both fell a sleep - me for an hour, Bob for about 3 hours. We've officially run out of things to do so I got the bags out this morning and we started practicing. I was a little nervous that Bob would get frustrated but he did awesome - of course. We started with short throws and within minutes, he was throwing them about 5 feet. Then I got nervous that we were going to hit the window or the TV. Those bags are actually pretty heavy so we only play for about 5 minutes and then we take a break.

We were able to eat lunch outside before the storms got here. I begged the aide to allow us to go out in the courtyard. We were the only ones there and it was a peaceful calm lunch. I have to say the staff is magnificent when it comes to specialty requests like that. Bob even sat long enough to enjoy a cup of coffee and some desert. My plan is to go outside as much as possible for everything. Hopefully we can get therapy to start doing some things outside. Something for me to work on next week. Praying for these pain-free comfortable days to continue for Bob! GO BOB!

MONDAY, MAY 30, DAY 110

What a magnificent day. Bob was so Bob today. He called me crazy again so I told him he was weird. Then I asked him if I'm crazy and he's weird then who's nuts and he said we both are...HA!

He has a great sense of humor and a fantastic attitude. I can tell already that he's going to need help with patience. He's anxious to get home so I keep telling him when he's strong enough and it's safe enough. So far, that line is working but pretty soon, I'm going to need new material! :) GO BOB!

TUESDAY, MAY 31, DAY 111

Bob tried to climb out of bed this morning. His pillow and sheet fell on the floor and he wanted to get them. I walked in at 7 and that was the first thing I saw - Bob hanging over the edge. Yikes! Now I'm worried about him falling on the floor again. The good news is he's getting so strong we have to worry about these things! Big day Thursday. We're going out to a local park for a picnic. We're going with another patient and family, which I think will be good. There will be someone else in a wheelchair so hopefully Bob won't feel like everyone's watching him. It's a short 2 hour get-away but it will give Bob a great break in the routine of therapy, sleeping, eating - therapy, sleeping, eating - repeat.

Bob's personality is starting to shine through. His crazy sense of humor, his driving work ethic and physical capabilities are all coming together. He's a super hero rock star!!!!! GO BOB!

JUNE 2011

WEDNESDAY, JUNE 1, DAY 112

Bob walked using the parallel bars today...TWICE! That means he walked without the walker. He holds on with his left hand and walks between the bars, sits down for a rest while I back him up to start over. He had enough energy and enthusiasm to do it two times. He's amazing. Speech therapy started working with him for two sessions today too - once in the morning and once in the afternoon. He did great. He was one worn out guy tonight and only made it thru dinner. No cards tonight. He just wanted to lie down. He was only up for about an hour and went back to bed at 6:30. He was already dozing about a minute after lying down. Big day tomorrow. We're going to the park for a picnic...WOO HOO! Can't wait. I'm pretty sure I'm more excited than Bob although after I told him he got to skip most of his therapy tomorrow, he perked up a little :)

THURSDAY, JUNE 2, DAY 113

What a beautiful day! We went on our picnic with two other families. We had a great time. I remembered the sunscreen, thank goodness. We enjoyed the new park on Reed's Lake. It is completely handicap accessible right down to the picnic tables. PERFECT! We spent 2 hours at the park and got back around 1:30. Bob normally has therapy at 1:30 so I expected it would be canceled but they were waiting at the front door as soon as we got back. He had a really big day and was completely exhausted by 6:30. He powered thru dinner and then had a shower. He asked for some pain meds and was pretty much fast asleep by 7:00. I sure hope he has a restful sleep tonight. At least he has only one more day of therapy and then the weekend. They moved him from his private room into a semi-private last night. Would have been nice to know. I walked in this morning and his room was empty. They told us he was going to move but we didn't know when. Gotta love the communication in the medical field. Things like this make me really, really crabby. But on a good note, that means Bob is progressing so well he doesn't need a private room anymore. His new roommate is very quiet and I think it will be fine for Bob. I'm just irritated on how the move took place. GO BOB!

FRIDAY, JUNE 3, DAY 114

Must be going to the park was just the ticket. Bob had a great day. He was wide awake this morning and ready to go. He walked the parallel bars again and did it pretty much all by himself. This afternoon, he walked down the hallway with the walker. On Monday, he's going to try walking down the hallway with just the railing on the wall. That should be really exciting. It's still rather painful to walk so he needed some more good drugs this afternoon. He asked the nurse himself. It's WONDERFUL to see how independent he's becoming. I'm so very glad he can communicate what he needs. I sleep better at night knowing he can let people know when he needs something. He's still really skinny but he now weighs 161 pounds. That's four pounds more than 2 weeks ago. At least he's going in the right direction. I told him we both need to gain 20 pounds so we're going to eat more ice cream and cookies in the afternoon. Praying for a pain-free restful weekend for Bob!

MONDAY, JUNE 6, DAY 117

Bob asks to come home every day now. It tears at my heart. I would love to just jump in the car and take him home, throw the covers over our heads and just pretend this never happened. Hopefully his next outing will be a day trip to the house. I'm not sure that would be a good thing or a bad thing. I'm sure he won't want to go back.

He's eating really well and can eat whatever he wants. He also eats in the general dining room now. I told him he has "first" seating just like on our cruises. "Second" seating is always later and we always had to wait for our food in the low stim dining room. He does just fine with all the activity in the general dining room and eats everything they give him. We also snack on cookies, M&Ms, ice cream and pudding in the afternoon. He gained another 2 pounds - thank goodness! He now weighs a whopping 163. I finally took an hour off today and got my hair cut. Last cut was in March. My loving brother told me I looked like bride of Frankenstein. At least he was nice enough to tell me my new hair cut looks good :) GO BOB!

TUESDAY, JUNE 7, DAY 118

4 months ago today unfortunate circumstances came together and changed our lives forever. Bob survived an unbelievable accident and is now thriving in rehab. He is truly a miracle and we are incredibly blessed. He has a great sense of humor and makes the therapists laugh on a daily basis. One of them

is very short and Bob is 6'2." Today she told him to bend over her shoulder while he was standing so he could get a good stretch in his back. He took one look at her and said, "Man are you short." His ability to endure the therapy sessions and still say "thank you" after each one is a testament to his strong conviction toward recovery. While we know he will forever have limitations with his right side and his speech is difficult right now, he has progressed leaps and bounds beyond my wildest expectations. In fact, I have no expectations which is what makes every day amazing to me!

He's a super hero rock star and continues to strive to be the best Bob he can be. GO BOB!

WEDNESDAY, JUNE 8, DAY 119

Another amazing day. Bob is doing great. This morning he was up and at it by 7:15 in the bathroom washing his face, brushing his teeth and shaving. These are all normal things that we take for granted during our morning routines. Bob was able to finally do normal things for himself. He is very resourceful and figures out how to work with just his left hand. It was great to see him regain some independence. Tomorrow he will tackle putting on a shirt. He also walked down the hallway using just the handrail. I wish I could describe the look on his face and how it made me feel. He was BEAMING! I was pinching myself so I wouldn't cry again :) He walked 78 feet by himself with just a little help with his right leg. HE'S INCREDIBLE! Every day he surprises me with his abilities. GO BOB!

FRIDAY, JUNE 10, DAY 121

Bob walked 150 feet today down the hallway. He wasn't even breathing hard this time. It was so cool to see. People are so encouraging and always stop to just watch. It really is awe-inspiring. Bob just strolls along with a big smile on his face. IT'S AWESOME! He also continues to work really hard with his speech therapist. He has such a sense of humor it's fun to see. She asked him if a refrigerator is hotter or colder than fire. He said colder and then said, "you should know that." HA! :) He's so intent on joining conversations that he talks a little bit to fast. We just remind him to slow down and he does much better. We had cookies this afternoon and brownies this evening. I sure hope we can add some pounds to him. He's burning off everything he eats and he eats really well. How come it's easy to gain weight when you don't want to and hard when you do?

Praying for a safe and restful weekend. Bob seems to get in trouble around Sunday morning. He gets bored and then looks for things to do. Last Sunday he tried to get out of bed so now he has a bed alarm and a tab alarm. Today the therapists showed him how to wheel his own wheel chair. I have visions of Bob racing down the hallway and out the door. I'm sure he'll need a chair alarm at some point. GO BOB...wait... STAY IN BED BOB!

MONDAY, JUNE 13, DAY 124

It was a rather long weekend for Bob. He didn't sleep well Saturday night so he ended up sleeping most of Sunday. He even had lunch in bed. He hasn't ever done that. He's now on a muscle relaxant for his right side and I think he just needs to get used to it. Today was much better with therapy and a schedule. He managed to work his way thru everything. He wasn't too keen on getting up for supper but as his usual self, he found the energy to eat and we even spent some time outside. During our evening chat, he told me that "this sucks big time" and I told him I completely agree. Then he said, "I know one thing. I need to be more careful." While he doesn't remember the accident, he knows he had one and he's trying to figure out what the heck happened. After all, it was February when this happened and now for him it's all of a sudden June. We're talking about a different wheel chair again. Now we're going to have one that is "normal" - whatever that means. I guess it has a lower back and it's a lot lighter. He'll be able to wheel himself around. All good things. Progress, progress, progress. It's wonderful and terrifying at the same time. He needs to be safe! GO BOB!

SUNDAY, JUNE 19, DAY 130

Wow...I can't believe I haven't posted since Monday. A lot happened this week. Bob is doing unbelievably well. His speech therapy is going great. He is talking up a storm and it's wonderful. His comprehension continues to amaze me. Today he told me he gets confused and I said that's OK because I do too. Then he said, 'yea, but you're confused all the time' and laughed. HA! He's just a regular comedian. He says hi to all the people we pass in the hallway and today he thanked a guy for moving out of the way. I love that he is so aware of his surroundings. Thursday, he started the E-Stim machine on his right arm and let me tell you that is the worst thing EVER! They hook him up to electrodes that stimulate the muscles in his arm. He says it doesn't hurt. It just feels weird. The bad part is as the machine is stimulating the muscles; the therapist is stretching them as well. OUCH! His words, "that's frickin' awful." He also told the therapist "you're killin' me." Horrible to see but after 2 treatments, his arm and hand already look more relaxed and he says they don't ache as much. Glad to know it's working but horrible to see the pain he has to endure. We had a sleep-over Saturday night. Spectrum was great to allow me to stay. Bob fell asleep at 7:30 and had a great nights rest. I, on the other hand, got absolutely no sleep. Too worried about something happening. Yes I know it's stupid to worry. Nothing happened and it was great to be with him through the night. Now I know the noises and interruptions he goes thru every night. I'm surprised he gets any sleep at all.

Looking forward to another great week. Now that our internet works again, maybe I can find the time at night to let everyone know what's happening. Thanks for the continued prayers and support. Bob is my hero and he's an amazing individual. We are truly blessed. GO BOB!

TUESDAY, JUNE 21, DAY 132

Bob's learning to walk with a platform walker now. His right arm rests on a little padded "arm" on the walker while his left arm moves the walker forward. He also has a brace that fits into his shoe that helps with the right ankle. He is already walking so much better and stronger this week and it's only Tuesday! LOVE IT!

When he's not in therapy or sleeping, he's bored. I keep telling him it's good to have break times and just laying in bed resting is just as good as lying in bed sleeping. As soon as he wakes up he's ready to go. He's never been a TV watcher so just laying in bed IS really boring. I'm talking with the recreational therapist tomorrow to see if there are fun things to do during Bob's "rest" times. His therapy schedule has changed a bit again. He has the dreaded E-STIM torture device on his right arm at 3 now. That means they added a third occupational therapy session, which is good but bad. It's good for Bob's rehab but bad because it's so painful. Rehab ain't for the faint of heart that's for sure.

THURSDAY, JUNE 23, DAY 134

Bob had an awesome day. Speech therapy this morning was hilarious. The last thing he does is answer 10 yes and no questions. Going into the last question, he had all the answers correct. Therapist said he would have 100% if he answered the last question correctly. He said, "make it easy." It was and he scored 100%. YAY! He walked again today and this time he used a cane-type thing with four feet on the bottom and just one handle for his left hand. HE DID AWESOME! He's getting so strong. You can see the muscles coming back and they're beautiful, I must say. He'll have his "guns" back in no time. This afternoon the therapy pets stopped by and they absolutely love Bob. The dog owner said her dog has never been this excited to see someone. Bob loved it. It was a nice distraction before the dreaded e-stim machine a.k.a. torture device.

He had quite a bit of pain this morning and required the good drugs, which he hasn't needed since last week. He was also rather restless this afternoon and only slept for about 30 minutes. After dinner we played some cards until about 7 and then he fell asleep. I sure hope he sleeps well tonight. Only one more day and then the weekend. He's earned some time off. GO BOB!

MONDAY, JUNE 27, DAY 138

Bob started a new pain reliever yesterday called Neurontan... or something like that. It's for nerve pain. He is in constant pain on his right side from his shoulder to his toes. He's sick and tired of it and I don't blame him. I can't begin to imagine what he's going through right now. Not only is he in pain but the therapists constantly work that right side. I'm hoping that this new drug will give him some good relief soon.

He also has a new bed. The nurse told him he will probably feel like he's camping because the bed goes almost all the way down to the floor. They put mats along the side of the bed so if Bob climbs out, he'll fall on the mats. Yesterday, he was lying on his stomach on the side of the bed trying to close the curtain between him and his roommate because the light was in his eyes. He wasn't really trying to climb out but it showed everyone that he definitely has the strength to do it. His weight is still an issue and he's stuck at 160...actually he fluctuates between 159 and 160. Feeding tube can't come out until he gains about 10 pounds. He eats really well and I'm not sure how to get any more calories into the man. Dietician told me that his metabolism will stabilize and he'll eventually gain weight. Bob is anxious to come home and he's "sick and tired of it." He has a bit of work to do yet and I'm praying for patience for both of us. Also praying for pain free days to come soon. GO BOB!

TUESDAY, JUNE 28, DAY 139

Bob had a pretty good day today. We remembered the pain pills around 1:00 pm and it seemed to do the trick for the afternoon. He had some more Tylenol just before dinner and he seemed to be much more comfortable. Now we just have to remember to do that every day. I visited Mary Free Bed today and what an awesome place. Bob would get about the same amount of therapy he has now but so many more options it's amazing. They have a really warm swimming pool that helps people with tone, like Bob, and will help him relax those muscles. The rooms are huge compared to where he is now. He would still have a roommate but with the space in the room, it wouldn't be a problem. I explained to Bob that the next step in his rehab is most likely to go to Mary Free Bed. He's OK with it because he understands it's one step closer to home. We'll be talking with the doc next Thursday July 8. We have some decisions to make and I'm praying for guidance. It's about Bob and we just need to make sure he has all the tools available to continue to be the best Bob he can be.

He's remarkable and continues to endure each day as it comes. We are truly blessed! GO BOB!

THURSDAY, JUNE 30, DAY 141

Bob's been accepted into the Mary Free Bed Brain Injury Program! WOO HOO! Scary and wonderful. The plan is to move on Tuesday July 5 but y'all know how that goes so it will definitely happen and we're aiming for Tuesday. Phase I - Borgess NCU February 8 Phase II - Borgess PIP March 15 Phase III - Spectrum Health Rehab April 5 Phase IV - Mary Free Bed And so Phase IV of Bob's journey begins. GO BOB!

JULY 2011

SATURDAY, JULY 2, DAY 143

Sleepy day for Bob. He got up and in his chair about 6:30 this morning because he just didn't want to be in bed anymore. He ate breakfast around 8, went back to bed about 8:20 and slept until about noon. He got up for lunch and went back to bed about 1:30. Slept until about 5 and then got up for a shower, dinner and back to bed. Both his muscle relaxant and nerve pain meds were increased this week and they have totally knocked him out. He worked really hard this week too and I think it all caught up to him. Thankfully, his pain was being managed well today so he could sleep. I have to give my brother a special thank you for all that he is doing for both me and Bob. There is no way we could be doing this without him. Laundry, dishes, cooking, house cleaning, grocery shopping, lawn mowing, cat poop scooping...you name it he does it. He even bakes my gluten free bread so he can make a sandwich for me every day. He also took every one of Bob's socks and put Bob's name on them so we wouldn't lose them at Spectrum. He's amazing! I can't imagine what the cat litter would look like by now if he weren't here :) We started saying our good-byes to the weekend staff today. They are all so supportive and excited for Bob it's wonderful. They've done so much for us in the past 3 months it's impossible to put into words how much we appreciate them. GO BOB!

SUNDAY, JULY 3, DAY 144

Another nice lazy day. Bob was all about the Sunday afternoon nap today. He woke up at 4am this morning and they said he didn't really go back to sleep. He got up in his chair when I got there and we went to breakfast. Then he did the standing frame for 17 minutes - an all time record! YAY! I think the sleep and relaxation yesterday was perfect for him. He slept the afternoon away and then ate dinner in bed. I sure hope he sleeps tonight. Getting ready for the big move in 2 days. Bob is ready too. Change is good...right? Let's face it, change is scary!

MONDAY, JULY 4, DAY 145

Happy Independence Day! Bob is ready for the big move tomorrow. He's looking forward to a bigger room and eating
meals in his room. He knows that Mary Free Bed is one step
closer to coming home. He helped me pack up his room today and carry stuff out to the car. I'm not sure how in the
world we accumulated so much stuff in such a small space
but we did.

For those of you who aren't familiar with Mary Free Bed
(MFB), it's been around for 120 years and has just 10 beds
for traumatic brain injury patients. It's one of the top rehab
centers in the country. We are incredibly fortunate that Bob
has made so much progress and continues to have so much
potential that he qualifies for MFB. His drive and determination WILL make him the best Bob he can be.

Now that Bob is moving away from requiring so much medical care, we are entering an even more physically demand-
ing phase of Bob's journey. I'm praying he can handle the
increased demands and work thru the pain. GO BOB!

TUESDAY, JULY 5, DAY 146

Well, we got stuck at Spectrum for one more day. We'll be
moving tomorrow at 11 am. Too much paperwork. Good
thing we're used to all the extra background crap that goes
with the medical industry.

Bob's had 4 days of pretty much all rest and little work. He's
going bonkers from all the down time but it's made a HUGE
difference in his energy level and ability to communicate. We
had spectacular conversations today. It was awesome. Mary
Free Bed here we come!

WEDNESDAY, JULY 6, DAY 147

So far so good for moving at 11. One of the physician assistance stopped in to say everything is all set. Been here 3 months and never saw her before. At MFB Bob will be seen by the doc every day...YAY! I'm typing this by phone and I have 40-something eyes so please forgive any typos. Hope this site works at MFB. I guess we'll find out soon enough.

STILL WEDNESDAY

We finally made it to MFB. Left Spectrum at noon...an hour late because our social worker somehow sent the AmbuCab to Metro Hospital. What a nice way to end our stay at Spectrum. Anyway...moving on!

Bob was in his room and eating lunch by 12:30. After that we met the admissions nurse, admissions clerk, physicians assistant, nurse for days, nurse for nights, social worker, physical therapist and person from food service for tomorrow's meals. Bob was exhausted!!!!! Here's the coolest thing for today. MFB has one nurse aide that stays IN THE ROOM with the patients all the time. That's 24/7, every shift, all day. LOVE IT! I was very concerned that Bob would wake up tonight and wonder where he is. Now I will rest easier knowing that someone is there with him. Today the aide was Marvin and he's wonderful. I stepped out of the room for a moment and when I came back, Marvin had arrived and was chatting with Bob about fishing. It is a HUGE relief to have someone with the patience and knowledge to wait for Bob to finish what he's saying and to listen closely enough to understand. We've only been there about 7 hours and already I feel more relaxed. Let's hope this feeling continues. Big day tomorrow. All the therapists will be evaluating Bob's progress to determine his therapy regime. I'm tired just thinking about it! GO BOB!

THURSDAY, JULY 7, DAY 148

What a fantastic day. Bob adjusted without any issues. He had so much energy today he plowed through all his therapies with energy to spare. MFB doc adjusted Bob's meds so he's not getting them all at once. Now that they've spread out the pain and muscle relaxant drugs, he's doing great. He also had 3 days of rest and really not much therapy until today so he was ready to go. Bob is amazing. How he endures the hours of therapy is beyond me. He met a bunch of new people today and did a bunch of new stuff without any hesitation. He's still my super hero rock star and always will be. GO BOB!

FRIDAY, JULY 8, DAY 149

Bob had a really busy day today and not much rest. He was really restless this evening and adamant about going home. He had a shower about 6:30 and then finally fell asleep about 7. He's been sleeping ever since...thank goodness. So far, MFB is the best place ever. The fact that someone is with Bob 24/7 is outstanding. My worry factor has been cut in half. In fact, there's a nice note in the room for family that says thank you for helping to take care of your loved one but if you leave the room for anything, make sure to tell the aide. They don't want the patients to be by themselves for even 10 seconds. PHEW! Bob's coordination isn't quite what he thinks it is and getting out of bed is rather easy for him. He just wouldn't be able to stand up once he got out. Instead of putting alarms on everything and giving him a bed that is pretty much on the floor, they make sure an actual human is watching him all the time. It's hard to describe how wonderful that is. Bob deserves the best and he's getting the best at MFB.

Today marks 5 months since the accident. What an unbelievable journey. Crazy where life takes you.

> February 8 - Borgess NCU March 15 - Borgess PIP April 5 - Spectrum Health SubAcute Rehab July 6 - Mary Free Bed Acute Rehab We give thanks everyday for the incredible network of family, friends, neighbors and coworkers that are helping us along. Your prayers and support are greatly appreciated! GO BOB!

SATURDAY, JULY 9, DAY 150

Ooops...not sure why that posted twice but at least we know it works. YAY! I found the free coffee too! This place just keeps getting better and better.

This morning Bob walked with the Eva walker again so the new physical therapist (PT) could evaluate his abilities. This is the best he has ever walked. He moved both legs all by himself...ABSOLUTELY NO HELP FROM ANYONE...and walked 100 feet. It was AWESOME! The therapist kept quiet and only gave Bob encouragement liked "nice step" and "that was perfect." He also listened closely to what Bob was telling him and he made a few adjustments with Bob's right arm so it was more comfortable. What a HUGE HUGE HUGE difference in just one session. I'm so proud of Bob and his accomplishments I just don't know what to do with myself! I could run around with my tongue sticking out but that's so old school now :)

I wonder what amazing things Bob has in store for this afternoon...

SUNDAY, JULY 10, DAY 151

Yesterday afternoon Bob had a really tough speech therapy session. They pushed him to his limit and then beyond. He was really riled after that session but we went to the gym for more PT, which seemed to settle him down a bit. We're battling the wheelchair again this weekend too. Still trying to find one that fits his long willowy legs!

The report this morning said both Bob and his roommate Tim had a very good night. They slept soundly...YAY! Bob was just waking up when I arrived. He ate breakfast about 7:45 and now fast asleep again. Therapy starts at 10 so he has some time to rest. He has a really light day today for therapy so hoping he gets lots of rest. I'm positive that next week is going to wear him out!

PS: he shaved his beard off! He hasn't been without some type of beard for 20 years. He asked the night nurse tech to help him so now it's all gone. He looks about 18 years old. I'm going to need a face-lift to keep up with his anti-aging process!

SUNDAY NIGHT

Bob had an OK afternoon. His right arm was bothering him after therapy and his room was kinda warm. I think he was uncomfortable and just couldn't figure out what to do about it. He had some pain meds about 4:00 and settled in for an afternoon nap. He also takes a shower tonight so hopefully that will help him relax and sleep well. I think the therapists are done with their evaluations so next week is going to be a busy get-down-to-business kinda week. Bob is all about being busy so I hope he knows what he asked for. No more being bored! :) GO BOB!

MONDAY, JULY 11, DAY 152

Bob's schedule is cram packed today!!! Holy crap! This afternoon might be a tough one. He's going to be tired and incredibly restless by the time 4:00 rolls around. I hope that doesn't happen but that's been the trend. I know in my head that this is the best thing for him but in my heart I just want him to lay in bed and sleep. It doesn't help that it's a rainy thundering morning. Right now, both Bob and his roommate are enjoying a little nap before all the ruckus of therapy starts. Praying for a pain-free uneventful day. GO BOB!

MONDAY EVENING

Bob had a great day and made it all the way through every therapy. He's getting stronger and stronger. Marvin is his nurse tech again tonight. He and Bob have bonded. It's also great to see how Bob is bonding with the therapists. The recreational therapist's name is Brie, like the cheese. Bob said she talks too much. :) I can't imagine what he says about me since I talk non-stop pretty much all day long. This is a wonderful, wonderful place. In just 5 short days, Bob has really blossomed. Today he got fully dressed with absolutely no help. Try stiffening up your right arm and leg and then putting on shorts and a t-shirt using only your left hand. After that, try putting a sock on your right leg while it's stiff and not cooperating; again using only your left hand. I have no idea how Bob figures these things out but he did today and it was marvelous! I LOVE HIS INDE-PENDENCE! GO BOB!

WEDNESDAY, JULY 13, DAY 154

Another busy day for Bob. Speech starts at 8 and then he's busy until 11:00. This afternoon he has 3 more therapy sessions and then rest at 3:00pm. Phew! I'm tired just looking at his schedule. Pray for pain management, a good attitude and strength for Bob to plow thru the day. GO BOB!

WEDNESDAY EVENING

BOB HIT GOLF BALLS TODAY!

GO BOB!

TUESDAY, JULY 19, DAY 160

Somebody count the days for me. I think I lost track :)

BOB'S FEEDING TUBE IS GONE!!!!! HOLY CRAP!!!!

This morning the nurse came in to change the bandage and Bob said it's gone. They took it out last night. We both looked at him and said we didn't think so but hopefully it will come out soon. She lifted his shirt and holy crap!!! IT'S GONE!!! We both apologized for about 5 minutes for not believing him. I feel bad for not believing him and incredibly ecstatic about the tube being gone!!!!! THAT WAS THE LAST PIECE OF EQUIPMENT...WOO HOO!

STILL TUESDAY

Thanks for counting. At this point, maybe I can just say "Day 161 give or take..." :) Found out today that this Friday, Bob will have surgery on his right foot. The goal is to improve his mobility and hopefully reduce long-term pain. He'll be non-weight bearing on his right side for 2 weeks. The good news is he'll be able to continue therapy; he just won't be walking for 2 weeks. We're looking at this as a plateau rather than a set back. It just puts us even for 2 weeks. No big deal. Bob asked some great questions and he was the one that made the final decision to have the surgery. His goal in his words..."to get from here to there faster." The surgery will definitely help him achieve this goal. Prayers for a successful surgery with minimal pain. GO BOB!

WEDNESDAY, JULY 20, DAY 162

2 weeks ago today we arrived at MFB and today Bob walked without the aid of a walker - only 2 therapists holding him on either side. SHOCKINGLY AMAZING!!! It was beautiful. I'm so glad we are here and not that other place. Bob has progressed by leaps and bounds in just 10 days. It's truly mirac-

ulous what he's accomplished, not only in the past 5 months but in just the past 2 weeks. He continues to be my super hero rock star! GO BOB!

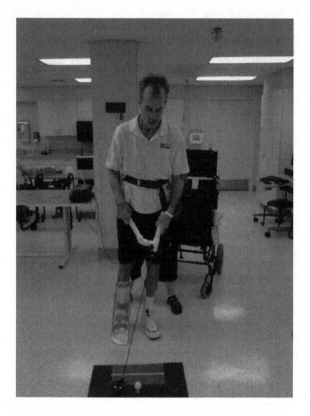

THURSDAY, JULY 21, DAY 163ISH...I THINK

Bob is amazing. His Neuroton was increased again yesterday and he is wiped out. Despite being incredibly tired, he walked FOUR TIMES around the hemi-bars with only minimal assistants. VERY, VERY COOL! (Hemi-bars are like parallel bars but they make an oblong circle so you can just keep walking around and around). He was pooped when he got done but pushed thru it and did awesome during speech therapy. More therapies this afternoon. I sure hope he can make it thru. He's wiped out! GO BOB!

SATURDAY, JULY 23, DAY 165

Surgery went well yesterday. Took about 2 hours. Bob's right foot is straight and flat. He was pretty sleepy and rested the remainder of the day. He had a good dinner and then slept thru the night.

Today he was in a bit of pain and not very comfortable. He still did awesome in therapy. He had 2 speech therapy sessions, one OT and one PT. Amazing what he can endure. He was a bit confused, agitated and restless this afternoon. Couldn't find a comfortable position and the big ol' cast on his right foot didn't help. Finally fell asleep about 3 and was snoring away when I left. Marvin is his aide tonight and Marvin knows how to keep Bob comfortable and calm. It's wonderful to know Bob is in good hands. I'll still have to call tonight just to make sure all is well. I just gotta know so I can sleep. Things piled up at home and it was time for me to take a few hours and get caught up. I'm already feeling rejuvenated. Just getting the 4 months of junk mail off the kitchen table made me feel better. Plus I had to organize all Bob's medical papers. Geez...the medical industry will never go paperless, I can tell ya that much! Working on a wheel chair for Bob that will allow him to keep his right foot elevated for the next 2 weeks. I'm praying for a successful recovery from foot surgery that allows Bob more mobility and less pain. That would truly be a miracle! GO BOB!

MONDAY, JULY 25, DAY 167

Bob is doing super fantastic. He had to stay in the room again today because he doesn't have a wheelchair that will keep his right leg elevated. He's been sitting in his chair with his foot propped up on the garbage can with a pillow. At 3:00, we finally got a new chair. Hopefully tomorrow we can go out and see people again.

Doc came in about 11am and started reaming on Bob's right arm. It was awful and I wanted to punch him. He's about 5'6", 130# and wears a bow tie. I'm pretty sure I could take 'im! He's a magnificent doc and excellent at what he does. He's done so much for Bob I can't begin to find the words to thank him. I would recommend him over and over again to anyone that needs a physiatrist. However, just be aware that what needs to be done isn't always pleasant to see or to feel, I'm sure!

Even though Bob spent the day in his room, he had oodles of therapy. He did great and continues to make unbelievable progress every day. He's truly amazing, as is Mary Free Bed! GO BOB!

THURSDAY, JULY 28, DAY 170

Bob continues to speed down the rehabilitation highway! He's making unbelievable progress. Speech therapy is taxing and takes everything he's got but WOW what an amazing thing to see. What was difficult and frustrating last week is a piece a cake this week. Even the therapist was excited. Fist bumps and high fives all the way around!!!

Bob and I are learning how to transfer from chair to bed together and we're also learning how to maneuver his chair up and down curbs. Good thing I know how to lift with my legs and not my back. It's also a good thing he only weighs 160#! AND it's a good thing he does most of the work. I'm just there for support. He gave me a kiss right after we stood up together so I figured I must have done something right :) Now I have to go eat my Non-Wheaties (the gluten-free alternative). GO BOB!

FRIDAY, JULY 29, DAY 171

Bob has his cell phone back! I suspended service for the past few months and turned it back on today. He asked one of the nurse techs to call me Wednesday night so I figured it was time he had his own phone again. I left about 4:00 pm today to get some stuff done at home. He called me about 5 and wanted to know how things were going. Just your average husband phone call checking in with his wife to see what was up...ya know...no big deal! It was such a normal phone call I had tears in my eyes. I thought I was passed that! :) He's just full of surprises. GO BOB!

AUGUST 2011

MONDAY, AUGUST 1, DAY 174

Bob is Bob. I'm not sure how to explain this but over the past few days, Bob's personality has really blossomed. He has such a sense of humor the therapists aren't quite sure how to take him. He will say "ouch" before they even start doing stuff and then smile and say "just kiddin." Sometimes he'll say, "just practicin." Cracks me up to see the look on the therapists' faces. HA!

Yesterday morning was a little rough. He was frustrated and fed up with this "whole business." We were riding back up on the elevator after therapy and he told me for the zillionth time "this sucks." I finally just said to him "well ya know Bob it sucks for me too." As we got off the elevator he said, "I guess we just have to make the best of it." And so we are and we will. GO BOB!

TUESDAY, AUGUST 2, DAY 175

It is so wonderful to hear Bob's laugh again. It's a daily occurrence now for us to get the giggles. His stupid cast weighs about 10 pounds and keeps sliding down the footrest of his chair. We were going down the hallway today and I had to stop and fix it. While I'm doing that, Bob repositioned himself in his chair and down the cast went again. I put my hands on my hips, made a big "harrumph" sound, and said, "Oh Bob, I'm trying to help but I need to know what you're doing so I can help." Just as I said that the cleaning guy walked by and had this big surprised look on his face. Bob started laughing and talking at the same time and then I started laughing because it was so wonderful to hear him laugh. We were still laughing in the elevator. Ahh...it's good to laugh. Tomorrow the cast comes off and will be changed to something more functional like a boot or a brace. Hopefully Bob will be able to put weight on that foot again and start walking. Praying for quick healing and no pain on that foot! GO BOB!

WEDNESDAY, AUGUST 3, DAY 176

THE CAST IS OFF...WOO HOO! Bob's right foot looks awesomely normal. He has to wear a big walking boot all the time and can only take it off to shower. He wasn't real happy about having to sleep with it on but at least it weighs less than the 10 pound cast. He was up and standing on it this afternoon during therapy and said it felt pretty stiff and sore but he made it through. He's continues to be amazing. We also had the home evaluated to see what needs to be done to make it safe and functional for Bob. This is just the preliminary stuff and we still have to talk to the contractor who will actually manage the work. So far, it's not horrible but ya know how home renovations can go. You change one thing and it causes a big ripple affect and you end up changing 25 other things. I'm just thrilled and elated that we are actually talking about coming HOME!!!! No date yet but the simple act of planning for Bob's home coming is truly awe inspiring. Wow! Can it be that after 6 months we can actually entertain the idea of coming home???? SWEEEEEET! GO BOB!

THURSDAY, AUGUST 4, DAY 177

Bob walked around the hemi-bars today. He looked so good it was amazing. He was standing up straight and tall and didn't have any issues with his right foot. He was really tired after one pass but he did great!!!! We also practiced transfers in and out of a recliner and on and off the bed. He's so strong he doesn't really need me. It was great to see the big smile on his face when we were done. The therapist said we both did great. We both know the sooner we master the art of transfers, the sooner he can come home. Yay! It's like we have a renewed focus on why we're doing all this stuff. He's my hero! GO BOB!

SUNDAY, AUGUST 7, DAY 180

Bob and I mastered the art of transfers today. I'm now officially approved as his transfer buddy. He'll be able to get in and out of the chair when ever he wants with me. He also mastered the art of getting dressed. It only takes him about 10 minutes to get fully dressed, socks 'n all. He's remarkable! Lots of visitors and a light day of therapy...the perfect Sunday! A group of our good friends stopped by and it was so uplifting to see them. Bob was beaming and really enjoying himself. It was sooooo good to see him happy, smiling and participating in the conversation. We laughed about old times and joked about times to come. Emotional but in a good way. We are both so very thankful for our good friends, family and everyone seeing us through this journey. GO BOB!

MONDAY, AUGUST 8, DAY 181

Bob graduated to using a hemi-walker today. WOO HOO!!!! No more parallel bars. He walked 31 feet today on his own. But remember, as we have to remind Bob. it's about quality not quantity and his steps were beautiful. Of course, the therapist stands right next to him but she said she wasn't doing anything. She was just there for safety. IT WAS AWESOME! His arm is starting to hurt more and more. The Botox is wearing off. It will be 3 months Aug. 12 and it only lasts about 3 months. It hurts all the time and it's starting to tighten up again. More Botox in Bob's future. I think it's part of his anti-aging routine now☺ GO BOB!

TUESDAY, AUGUST 9, DAY 182

Holy crap Bob climbed four stairs today! First he walked 50 ft in the hallway with just his cane/crutch thingy and then he walked up four stairs AND back down again. Unbelievable! He's going to be walking into the house in no time. I'm so very very very happy for him! This afternoon we practice getting in and out of the car. I wonder how difficult that will be? I guess we'll find out shortly. This morning while he was standing to get into his chair, I banged my ear on his forehead. We both started laughing so he had to sit back down on the side of the bed. We ended up being late for therapy because we had to stop laughing before we could transfer to his chair. I can tell ya laughing is WAAAYYYY more fun than crying! GO BOB!

WEDNESDAY, AUGUST 10, DAY 183

Bob walked a quality 125 feet...WOO HOO! He also had to work in the kitchen. Nothing too strenuous. :) They have a model kitchen set up so people can practice. Bob was able to maneuver himself all around that kitchen, make himself a PB & J, pour himself a glass of milk, and clean everything up and put it in the dishwasher. We'll have to move a few things around in our own kitchen to be within Bob's reach but other than that, no biggie. Two contractors have been through to review the renovations for the house. What an experience this is going to be. More new stuff to figure out. Bob's always done this stuff so I just "call Bob." I can tell ya these people have a high standard to meet to live up to Bob's workmanship. AND they better know that Bob is going to have whatever it takes to make it easier for him to adapt to his new lifestyle. I have a feeling I'm going to be on the phone a lot. And so begins the dance with insurance companies, contractors and subcontractors.

THURSDAY, AUGUST 11, DAY 184

TARGET RELEASE DATE FOR BOB TO COME HOME IS AUGUST 31!!!! GO BOB!

MONDAY, AUGUST 15, DAY 188

Bob is doing great. Range of motion on his right shoulder has increased to ensure he doesn't lose any ground. Unfortunately, it is EXTREMEMLY painful. The good new is it's working. Today his right arm was much more relaxed. The scary part now is that Bob and I have to learn to do range of motion together. How can I possibly be asked to "hurt" my husband even if it is for the better? That's going to be one tough thing to wrap my head around. I just have to remember it has to be done to ensure Bob regains as much function and mobility in his right arm as possible. We can do this and we'll do it together. GO BOB!

SATURDAY, AUGUST 20, DAY 193

Only 11 more days until Bob's home coming...but who's counting :)

Bob had a phenomenal week. I think it's all this talk about home. He's more than ready and tells everyone that he's leaving August 31. There are a whole lotta things that have to come together to make that happen - home renovations, medical equipment (I call these Bob's accessories) and medical support at home. The home renovations start Monday. The accessories were just ordered on Friday. We have to figure out how much support Bob will need at home so we know when to have the RNs visit us. Not to worry. We have 11 days.

As for Bob, he walks pretty much on his own at this point using what's called a hemi-walker. It has four feet with a handle at the top and he uses it with just his left hand. He will do just fine at home walking from the living room to the bedroom and any point in between. I'm just his spotter at this point. His speech is beautiful! He's very aware of the words that seem to come out not quite right and is able to correct them mid-sentence. That is a HUGE bonus for Bob and everyone is very excited that he recognizes that the words sound different and can correct them. He continues to work EXTREME-LY hard and a few of the therapists wanted to know if he's a perfectionist. I would say yes but only in a good way. He really wants to do the best he can at everything and it shows every day. He continues to amaze me with his ability to accept whatever they throw at him. I can't even imagine what it's like to work so hard every day with only a slight break on the weekends. He's truly miraculous!

Praying for everything to fall into place to allow Bob a smooth home coming on August 31. GO BOB!

WEDNESDAY, AUGUST 24, DAY 197

Bob and I spent the afternoon at Reed's Lake (with 3 therapists too but I think they just wanted to go so they could enjoy some time outside). Went fishin', had ice cream and strolled around the pathways by the lake. What a beautiful afternoon. It recharged our batteries. Bob usually takes a nap in the morning but no nap today and he's just resting in bed watching TV right now. I LOVE HOW MUCH ENERGY HE HAS NOW!!!!!

Home renovations are done enough for Bob to come home. The complete renovation will be done probably sometime in October but we'll make due until it's completely done. Bob's new lifestyle will be easy and enjoyable and we're going to make sure he has everything he needs to make it that way. GO BOB!

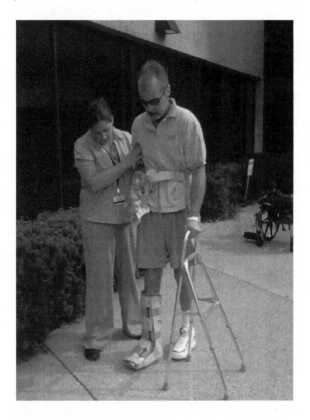

MONDAY, AUGUST 29, DAY 202

BOB COMES HOME IN 2 DAYS!!!!!! WOO HOO!!!!!

Bob had his second round of Botox in his right arm on Thursday last week and it's already working like a charm. He now helps with his own range-of-motion and that makes a HUGE difference. He's able to control the stretch and hold it himself. He knows when it hurts rather than a therapist yanking on it. He has come so far in such a short time it's awesome! Great write-up on the CEO of Mary Free Bed in Sunday's Grand Rapids Press. If you want to read it, here's the link:

> http://www.mlive.com/living/grand-rapids/index.ssf/2011/08/profile_mary_free_bed_ceo_kent.html

I spent the day yelling at insurance companies and medical equipment providers. I believe everything will be delivered to the house tomorrow (Tuesday). Why can't people just help people? Our healthcare system would be 1/100th of the size it is if everyone just did what they were supposed to do. Geez! But enough about me... GO BOB!

SEPTEMBER 2011

SATURDAY, SEPTEMBER 3

I don't know how many days anymore....

WE'RE HOME! Very emotional home coming. We all cried happy tears. It was awesome. Bob loves the new front porch but can't wait to get rid of the ramp. I made a deal with him that after the ramp isn't used for one full month, we'll talk about taking it out.

The first night home was pretty rough. Not much sleep because of the new surroundings. Thursday night was much better and last night was great. We're working through the adjustment period and time will take care of that. Friday was a HUGE day for Bob. Up at 8am with a little nap around 10 and then off to outpatient therapy. We left the house at 11am and got back around 4pm. He was exhausted but wouldn't sleep because all the neighbors were out playing in their yards. We ate dinner around 5 and then he was out and about with the neighbors until nearly 8pm. He was wiped out. Fell asleep as soon as he hit the pillow and is still snoozing away at 7am Saturday morning. We are so blessed to be home and in our own surroundings. Bob has come a long way since those first few months and continues to make great progress. I'm praying that he and I can continue his progress at home. We have to continue his therapies together and I'm hoping we don't lose any of the great gains he's made. WE LOVE BEING HOME! GO BOB!

SATURDAY AFTERNOON

WE WENT ON OUR NEIGHBOR'S BOAT TODAY!!! WOO HOO!

Bob was determined and has been talking about the boat since we got home. I kept telling him "next year babe." Well... he wouldn't hear of it. Our friends from Chicago were just as determined as he was so nobody listened to me. I was out numbered. So...we pushed his chair right up to the edge of the dock (reason for panic #1) and the young muscle-bound son-in-law pretty much hoisted Bob up and plopped him in the boat (reason for panic #2). Then we motored around for a few minutes and came back (reason for panic #3). Muscle-bound son-in-law hoisted Bob up and plopped him back in his wheel chair on the dock (final reason for panic). I'm still trying to recover from the stress of it all. Meanwhile, Bob is sound asleep taking a nap. Oh...and by the way...I made Bob wear a life jacket. I'm such a wife. :) GO BOB!

MONDAY, SEPTEMBER 5, 2011

Big weekend for Bob. Lots of fun and outside on and off all day every day. Yesterday we had dinner with our neighbors in their backyard and it was chilly. Who knew fall was here already. Bob went to bed about 5:30pm for nearly an hour and then got up to watch some TV. Went back to bed about 8:30 and slept pretty much all night. No fans making noise, nice breeze in the house...finally a good night's sleep for both of us.

We're pluggin' away at our homework and are able to keep up with his therapies on our own. Walking in the house is a challenge with the big walking boot and our nicely padded carpet. He's done a great job walking though. It just takes a long time to get from one place to the next. The wheelchair is a challenge around some of the corners but we've managed that too. Planning a big trip out tomorrow to go to the shoe store. Bob really wants some good walking shoes. We'll see what tomorrow brings. GO BOB!

SATURDAY, SEPTEMBER 10

What a big week. Weds and Thurs were huge days for Bob. Up and at 'em early and all day at therapy and appointments. Foot doc approved the removal of that big ol' foot brace...FINALLY! Now we're just waiting for the in-shoe brace to be made and GOOD BYE BOOT! Bob can't wait. This week he's been sleeping really well. He keeps us all busy during the day. Not a big one for naps but will occasionally sit in his recliner for a few minutes to relax. He loves to be outside. Good thing we live on a private road with no traffic so we can push that wheelchair all over the place. We must do at least 5 miles a day. I thought I walked a lot BEFORE Bob came home...ha!

Today the neighborhood had a pig roast, played bags and then cards in the late afternoon. We were able to visit the party on and off throughout the day. Mom and Dad Kamps stopped by and gave free hair cuts to Bob and brother Jack. Then we took another walk-about and finally Bob laid down about 8:00 pm. We played hooky from our homework today and skipped the range-of-motion on Bob's right arm. However, we did play cards (great for the mind), exercised legs (great for flexibility) and socialized (great for getting back into the community). What is really amazing to me is how much Bob talks. I'm not kidding. It's like he's a chatty Cathy or something. Docs are actually amazed by this because typically people with aphasia don't talk much. They know they have difficulty with words so they pretty much don't bother. Bob is just the opposite. He'll say something and then say, "Wait, that wasn't right." That's exactly what the docs and therapists want him to do because that's how his brain will work through the aphasia. He's amazing, strong, determined, driven, motivated, handsome, and ALIVE! GO BOB!

THURSDAY, SEPTEMBER 22

So much has happened in the past 12 days I'm not sure where to begin. We've settled into a daily routine and our therapy schedule is set so we know what to expect each week. Bob continues to make great progress. He's using his right hand and arm more and more. Today he had to make his own lunch and eat with his right arm. He did amazingly well. It took him awhile but he did it!!!! He's also experimenting with a simple cane that has four rubber feet on the bottom. One more big step to walking independently. The therapists feel that with time and strength, he will be walking on his own unassisted. YAY!

As part of his therapy, he has to help around the house. He'll be folding laundry and dusting the tables this weekend. He'll also be making his own lunch. Not sure how he feels about it but I'm pretty excited :) Our new front door will be installed tomorrow. I'll have to let you know how Bob does with someone else doing work on the house. I'm a little concerned how Bob will feel about it. The builder is a very low key calm guy so I'm pretty sure all will go well.

We just won't be able to leave the house until the door is installed. That might be a bummer.

Looking forward to a restful but fun weekend. GO BOB!

OCTOBER 2011

WEDNESDAY, OCTOBER 5

Does anyone read this anymore? Bob is doing super fantastic and making progress every day. He had his one month out-patient progress report Monday and it was amazing!!! Just for some measurable gains - his left hand strength measured 58 pounds and now it's 85 pounds! The therapist said that was ridiculous in a good way. People usually make gains of 10 pounds or so. Bob gained nearly 30 pounds in strength!!! He's also walking with just a simple cane with four prongs on the bottom. No more hemi-walker. He needs minimal assistance to walk and just stand-by assistance for some transfers. It's exciting to watch. His speech therapy sessions are still challenging and frustrating but he does his best and makes it through each hour long session every time. It's been nearly 8 months since the accident and boy have we come a long way. We are so thankful to have each and every moment together. Lots of cliches fit this situation - live life to the fullest; take nothing for granted; live in the moment - you never really know what those mean until something like this happens. Each day is a blessing for sure. GO BOB!

SATURDAY, OCTOBER 8

Wow...I'll keep writing! I had no idea Bob was so popular :)

Bob goes to out-patient therapy 3 times a week and the drive to Grand Rapids is getting to be too much. It takes an hour by the time we load up the car and unload when we get there. We toured the Allegan therapy gym on Friday and it looks great. They offer the same options as Grand Rapids - speech, OT and PT for therapies. They work with neuro-rehab as well. AND it's only 6 miles from our house! Mary Free Bed is by far the best place and has the most experience with Bob's type of injury but man, the drive is just too much. We're scheduled to attend therapy thru January but with the winter coming and the amount of snow we get, we'd like to have the option of going to Allegan. We'll talk to the doc about it and see what he thinks. In no way do we want to hinder Bob's progress. Maybe we can do Allegan for 2 or 3 months and then go back to MFB. I talked with his current therapists and they even suggested taking a vacation from it all for a few weeks. Boy would that be nice.

Speaking of vacations (which then reminds me of umbrella drinks)-it was a gorgeous night last night so we sat outside in our driveway and chatted with Mike, Bob's brother. That made Bob want a beer something awful. Every night he asks if he can have a beer while we're playing cards. I told him I'll ask the doc if he can have just one but I already know what the answer will be. Oh well, it never hurts to ask. In the meantime, will someone have a beer for Bob and let us know how it tastes? GO BOB!

WEDNESDAY, OCTOBER 12

*&$#@!!!!! Insurance companies stink BIG TIME! Bob continues his phenomenal progress and the house continues to be a hindrance. Carpeting, no shower, small doorways - all adding to the frustration of getting around. I firmly believe that Bob's progress would be further along if the house had been renovated b/4 we got home. However, the alternative was to stay at MFB or move to another institution instead of coming home...um...NO! I'm thankful he's home but now pulling my hair out trying to get the insurance company to move on the house. Boo!

Thank you to everyone who had a beer for Bob. I'm officially making Friday and Saturday nights "Beer for Bob" nights. Feel free to participate if you'd like either both nights or just one. You could also have "Bourbon for Bob" or "Banana Daiquiris for Bob." Just make sure to share how good it tastes so I can pass it on! GO BOB!

SATURDAY, OCTOBER 22

What a great week for Bob!!!! During therapy, he walks without the aid of anything but the therapist holding on to him AND he walked up and down steps with just the use of the railing...WOO HOO! The therapist is confident that he'll be walking without anything by this winter and he'll be able to go up and down steps to the basement. He's been wanting to go down there since we got home. He also moves that right hand more and more. Thursday he was picking up nerf balls and dropping them into a basket. It was amazing to watch. During speech therapy, Bob works on all types of different puzzles. He worked on one that had me stumped but he got it with very little help. He still thinks he's being tested every week and I keep telling him that they need to make sure he can do all this stuff so he can work and drive again. He really wants to get out in his pick-up truck. I'm hoping that remains a motivator for him.

One of Bob's friends had knee surgery and is now going through therapy. He also uses a cane. I think it's made Bob work that much harder knowing that his friend is going thru something similar. They've bonded even more over their canes :) We visited his friend yesterday and Bob was able to walk up the steps and into his house. We played cards for a bit and then came home. What a great "normal" Friday activity. The bathroom has FINALLY been approved. Builder should be starting in the next 2 weeks. That means we have to leave the house for a week or so. We'll be staying in a hotel.

NOT LOOKING FORWARD TO IT AT ALL! Change in routine is hard for everyone but even more so for a head injury survivor. Praying that all goes well. GO BOB!

TUESDAY, OCTOBER 25

Bob is a miracle for sure! His memory is getting better and better. Yesterday morning the traffic report said one of the roads we take was going to be closed. I told him to help me remember to take a different way to therapy. When we pulled out of our driveway 5 hours later, he said, "remember not to go thru Wayland. The road is closed." I LOVE IT!!!!

As you know, he's all about having a beer lately. We pass the bar in the big town of Hilliards on our way to therapy everyday. He told me to stop and get a beer on our way. I told him he doesn't usually have beer on Mondays and that I really didn't want one. So he told me I need to "cut loose" once in awhile. HAHAHA! We also have fun with the attendants that work with Bob. There's one in particular who's a nervous sort. She drinks too much caffeine and takes caffeine pills so we mess with her all the time. Bob tells her to do a bunch of random stuff all at once and then we watch her scurry around like a nervous Nelly. It's hysterical. She went to close the cereal boxes yesterday and spilled a full box of Cheerios all over the floor. Bob and I couldn't help but laugh and then we had the giggles all morning. I don't think she appreciated that at all :)

Bob is approved to start therapy in Allegan starting Dec 5 - only 6 miles from home - and we're finally making headway on the bathroom renovations. That should start in the next week or so. Looking forward to a new bathroom and nice flooring that will help Bob get around in the house more easily. WOO HOO! I shouldn't get excited yet because nothing has started but at least we're getting closer! GO BOB!

THURSDAY, OCTOBER 27

Bob walked up and down a flight of stairs...TWICE! Holy crap! He was so happy he cried. That means he will soon be walking down to our basement and out the sliding glass door. He's been asking to do that since he got home. I'm so excited for him! He also sat on a bosu ball and practiced his balance while we played Connect 4. He whipped me AND worked on his core strength all at once. Just a few months ago, Bob couldn't even sit up on his own. WHAT A MIRACLE.

Today we practiced falling on the floor. Just in case something happens, we're prepared to get up together. He's so strong he doesn't really need me. As usual, I helped too much but what a relief to know that should something happen and it's only the two of us, we're prepared. I'm sure there's some deeper lesson in there about falling and getting up together... ah, the things you learn during therapy.

For his right arm, Bob continues to wear a wrist brace and a pinky brace on and off during the day. He asks for braces because he knows they will help improve the use of his right arm. It's so exciting to have him actively participate in his own therapy. He also asks for stuff to do at home during the weekend so we always go home with homework from the therapists. The puzzles we do for speech are brain teasers for sure.

We ran into two of our old roommates this week...one from Spectrum and one from MFB. It was wonderful to see their progress as well. Seemed like everywhere we went this week, we ran into someone we knew. The therapists said it was like we were famous or something. I think it means we've been in the system too long! Or maybe Bob is just that famous. Another great week for Bob! GO BOB!

NOVEMBER 2011

FRIDAY, NOVEMBER 4

This week was another banner week for Bob! We met with the social worker, who hasn't seen Bob in about 7 weeks. She said within 30 seconds, she could tell all the tremendous progress he's made. His speech is clearer and he's more aware of his surroundings. She told him his brain continues to heal and he is doing an outstanding job. Then one of his therapists told him his progress is one of the best she's seen and she's worked with MFB for nearly 20 years. It's heart-warming and encouraging to hear these things, even though we all know everyone is different, no brain injury is the same and we all just have to wait and see what the progress will be.

Last Saturday, Bob walked down the steps on our deck outside and in thru the sliding glass door to the basement. It was beautiful! He rested for awhile and then walked all over the basement and then back outside and up the steps. Awesome! Now he wants to go downstairs nearly everyday. Good thing the builder is coming soon to start modifications to the house, which includes making the inside basement steps safer for Bob to use.

Speaking of the builder - the bathroom renovations are scheduled to start November 21, the week of Thanksgiving. We'll be moving to a hotel Nov 20 to Dec 4. The builder thinks he'll be done much sooner but ya never know. With the way this has gone, I don't expect to be home before Dec 4. Then on Dec 5, Bob starts therapy in Allegan. We have a big few weeks coming up. I sure hope the hotel stay isn't too much and Bob is able to adjust to the new therapy routine. I'm freakin' out a little but try not to think of everything all at once. Simply living in the moment while being realistic and planning for the upcoming events is the best we can do. GO BOB!

MONDAY, NOVEMBER 7

Bob was part of a prototype trial of an arm mobilizer today. Very cool! It works by allowing his right arm to basically be weight-free so he can move it around and use it more. He had to sign a release form to be in a video. He's truly a star now! I asked the guy to send us something to let us know when the video comes out so I'll have to let you know. Can't wait to see Bob's cameo :)

It was a loooonnnggg day today. Has the time changed messed anyone else up? We were up at 6:30am, left for therapy at 9am and got home at 4pm. The prototype thingy was this morning at 10 but well worth the extra effort. Bob and I enjoyed lunch together in the hospital cafeteria and then he had two more hours of therapy. By the time we got home, I needed a nap and he was still ready to go. His energy level is crazy in a good way.

BTW: tomorrow, Tuesday November 8 at 6:45 pm will be nine months since Bob's injury and our lives changed forever. We are truly blessed by friends, family, neighbors and coworkers. Thank you to everyone for your continued thoughts, prayers, support, and well-wishes. GO BOB!

SATURDAY, NOVEMBER 12

Bob and I experienced our first physical fall to the floor on Thursday during therapy. He was stepping off the scale and his right foot slid forward sending his weight backwards and down he went. I feel horrible, horrible, horrible. I was holding on to him as best I could so I "placed" him on the floor and then I landed right next to him. Thank goodness no bruises or scratches and he didn't hit his head. He was more embarrassed then anything else. He also remembers the fall very well and was concerned that I was hurt. He was so sweet to ask how I felt the next day. It's a good thing that his memory works so well but I wish he could just remember the good stuff :) PS - I do have a huge bruise on my right arm...I have no idea from what. I think I hit a chair but it all happened so fast I can't remember. Last weekend Bob helped wash windows outside on our front porch. It's a gorgeous sunny day today so maybe we can get some more outside work done. We'll see how we feel. GO BOB!

MONDAY, NOVEMBER 14

Just one more week and we're off to the hotel. Nervous, anxious, happy...all that stuff. It will be quite the adventure. At least there will be things to do and places to go. Looking forward to some nice dinners out with just Bob. We plan to go to the mall to do some Christmas shopping too. Can you believe it's the holiday season already? CRAZY! Bob is doing super well. However, along with that comes awareness of his limitations and of course sadness. He just wants it all to get better and quite frankly, so do I. Praying for patients and perseverance for Bob. He always finds the motivation to do what it is they tell him to do and he works really hard at home too. I can't begin to imagine what it's like to have pain everyday but he pushes thru and keeps on goin'. He's amazing and continues to be my hero. GO BOB!

WEDNESDAY, NOVEMBER 16

Bob continues to make great strides...literally. Today he was harnessed in to a machine that allowed him to walk with a normal gait to feel what it was like if he stumbled or started to fall. The machine took some of the weight off his legs. He walked normally all around the gym AND he got on the treadmill for 3 minutes. I wish I could explain it better but just know that it was awesome. Then the therapists had him working on his balance by reaching for a ball and throwing it back to them. He had so much fun he was faking out the therapist and then throwing the ball to me. At one point, he held the ball up and made the little therapist reach for it. He was hysterical. It made me laugh so hard I cried. He told me this morning he hoped he was motivated enough to get thru therapy today. That is the first time he's ever talked like that. His attitude is changing for the better and he's starting to realize what he needs to do. IT IS TRULY AWESOME! We have help during the day and thank goodness we have one attendant that we really like. She was with us today and she and Bob were singing "Zippidy-doo-dah" and then laughing because it got stuck in my head so I whistled it all day long. Great...now I'm whistling it again! Anyway...my point is Bob told me I'm the sunshine of his life. I cried again :) Happy tears! GO BOB!

SUNDAY, NOVEMBER 27

We are having a great time in the hotel. It's wonderful to be close to everything. The mall is literally 2 minutes across the street and every restaurant known to man is right here. We've eaten out twice and finished our Christmas shopping. We are seriously reconsidering the whole "live in the boonys" idea. We really do live in the middle of nowhere.

Bob is also working really hard. He's been walking around the hotel halls every day. Yesterday and today he walked with me holding on to him from behind. He picked up his cane and just walked down the hall. It was AWESOME! We also play a ton of card games. The newest one is called "Blink." If you haven't played it yet, go get it. It's really challenging and a lot of fun. Bob beats me just about every time. It's a game of speed and I get too nervous. We are truly thankful for every minute of every day and are incredibly blessed. GO BOB!

PS: the house looks great. We were able to go home for the day on Thanksgiving and we love the progress so far. We hope to be home by this Thursday. It will be so nice to have a house that helps Bob be more independent. YAY!

MONDAY, NOVEMBER 28

The cold weather really isn't good for Bob. Today was an off day. He just couldn't get comfortable and didn't sleep well last night. We canceled his first therapy at 1:00 pm because he fell asleep about noon and I didn't have the heart to wake him up. He was able to do his 2pm and 3pm therapies and then we came back to the hotel, ate dinner and relaxed. He crawled into bed about 6pm tonight. There just isn't a good comfortable place to sit in this hotel room other than the bed so we watched the news and played some cards. It was kinda fun but I wish I could make his pain go away. It's just always there. That's really gotta suck! Praying for a better, more comfortable day tomorrow!

DECEMBER 2011

THURSDAY, DECEMBER 1

Hopefully our final day at the hotel...YAY! Paul, our builder would like us home around noon on Friday so we can do a walk-thru and let him know if we need anything changed. Jack's been sending pictures along the way and the shower looks bee-u-tee-ful! The laminate floors look great and the new basement steps are going to be much easier for Bob to maneuver. There's more work to be done (like A/C, path to the boat, update basement bathroom, etc) but we can be home for any of the additional work. NO MORE HOTEL STAYS! Bob's progress continues to be phenomenal. The MFB therapists are doing their final evals before Bob goes to Allegan for therapy. His right side has increased in strength 5 times in 3 months. His grip strength was 3.2# on Sept 1 and it's 14# on Nov 30. He moves his right leg just like you and me - lifting at the knee, marching, walking. All that progress in just 3 months is crazy. The therapists said they are sad to see him leave because he's making such great gains. We'll be back to MFB in the spring after the bad weather leaves Michigan. I sure hope we're doing the right thing. If his progress slows remarkably, then we'll have to come up with a plan B so we can get back to MFB sooner. I'm putting the cart before the horse. You'd think by now I'd know to stop "what if"-ing and just go with the flow! :) I will continue to work on that. GO BOB!

MONDAY, DECEMBER 5

We're home from the hotel!!!! Got back Friday around 1pm. The bathroom is awesome and the new laminate flooring allows Bob to travel everywhere throughout the house. It's so wonderful to see him getting around so much easier. This morning he went into the kitchen in his chair and then stood at the kitchen sink all by himself. No help from anyone!!!! He also walked down and then back up the basement steps INSIDE the house. I was a nervous wreck. We took pictures and you should see my face...HA :) Bob's all smiles.

We start therapy in Allegan at 1pm today. It's only 6 miles away. Bob has friends that went to therapy there as well and they keep telling him how much it helped them so he's looking forward to it. I know he's nervous because it's something new but I know he'll do just fine. GO BOB!

MONDAY NIGHT, DECEMBER 5

Bob's first day at Allegan was awesome! Therapists are all really nice and Bob was in great spirits. He had plenty of energy and made it thru all the tests without any issues. When we got home he wanted to know what we were going to do next. We ate dinner and now he's relaxing in his recliner getting a foot message by his attendant. I'm a little jealous. Tomorrow marks 10 months since Bob's injury. What an incredible journey we're on and he continues to amaze ME as well as everyone else. We are incredibly fortunate, thankful, blessed, and graced by the good Lord. Prayers are powerful!

SATURDAY, DECEMBER 10

We have a big day planned today. Making Christmas cookies and putting up decorations. The really cool thing is I told Bob yesterday what we were going to do today and he told me this morning what we're doing...HUGE memory break-th-ru!!! We've also been reminiscing (sp?) about vacations and things from the past and he remembers going on our cruises and going to Maine. He also remembers going to San Diego every February. Still not sure where the memory stops and then starts again but we'll get there. He's making connections and improving EVERY DAY! He loves going to Allegan for therapy and this week has been OUTSTANDING. He's made leaps and bounds of progress in just one week. He wrote my birthday date on a sticky note all by himself without having to copy the letters. Another HUGE break-thru!!!! He's been able to do his signature for over a month now but now he's starting to write other things too. I was so happy for him I had tears in my eyes. He told me I was weird. "Why would that make you cry? Everyone should be able to write." It's hard to find the words to describe these feelings but just know that he's a walking (literally) miracle for sure. GO BOB!

SATURDAY, DECEMBER 17

Bob is just doing fantastic. He has homework to practice writing. Just a few short weeks ago, he had a frustrating time with writing anything. Today he wrote his name, address, telephone number, AND birthday. He only needed a little bit of coaxing with the numbers. Everything else came out beau-tifully. It's still hard to find words to describe the incredible progress he's made and continues to make. Three months ago he didn't know our address or telephone number. Now he rattles them off like nothin'!!!!

Today we got at least 2" of snow. This morning Bob was pretty insistent about walking out to the car to run errands. I told him it was too snowy and I was nervous about him slipping. He told me to "get over it." I told him I appreciated his enthusiasm but I was just too worried about it. In the end, he wheeled himself out to the car. He still listens to me on occasion.

We went to the furniture store to pick out his new recliner. He was able to walk around the store and try out a few recliners to see what would fit. He's just so dang tall! We have to get a large, which has a taller back and sits up a bit higher. It also holds up to 375 pounds so he can gain some weight, too... hopefully not that much though. We are incredibly blessed and have so much for which to be thankful (how's that for good grammar, ma? I didn't dangle my participle.). We truly enjoy every day and realize the great gift we've been given this holiday season. GO BOB!

TUESDAY, DECEMBER 20

Only two days of therapy this week and then a 6 day break! Bob doesn't have therapy again until next Wednesday. With the holidays, he has three weeks with only two sessions a week. He's asked each therapist what he can do at home to help with his progress. Of course every therapist was thrilled and gave him a mountain of homework. We have a file full of things to do. I'm so excited that he's participating so well in his own therapy. He's getting sick of it and keeps asking when he'll be done. I don't blame him one bit. Hopefully the holiday break will give him some time to relax and just enjoy some time away from scheduled therapy. GO BOB!

WEDNESDAY, DECEMBER 21

GO BOB Central! Today Bob told me he's sick of his chair and he's leaving it at home from now on so he walked from the house, down the steps and to the car. Then he walked from the car into therapy. We brought the chair just because therapy is 3 hours and I knew he'd be tired but I was so excited he wants to walk everywhere! After 3 hours of therapy, we came home and he rested for about 1/2 hour in his recliner and then came into the kitchen to help with dinner. He stood at the counter and told me what to do. It's a good thing because he's the cook of the family so I need all the help I can get. Yesterday, he stood in the kitchen and put away groceries!!!!! He even uses his right hand!!!! We're pretty excited in the Kamps household these days. GO BOB!

SATURDAY, DECEMBER 24

Merry Christmas Eve! Bob's latest amazing feat - he cleaned off the kitchen table and dusted it...while STANDING! There are three things that left me speechless:

> 1. I asked Bob if he would clean the table and he said, "sure." So he came into the kitchen, got the cloth, grabbed the pledge and went back to the table. All I said was, "Will you clean the table." He didn't need any other help with the process.
>
> 2. He's physically strong enough to stand and bend over to clean the table. AWESOME! Of course someone is always standing next to him because we practice "Safety First" in our household but the fact that he can physically do that is incredible.
>
> 3. The man hates to dust!

After he did the table, he sat back down and wheeled himself into the living room to dust off two more tables! I'm still speechless. He is my Christmas gift and that's all I need. He's made my season not to mention my entire year! GO BOB and MERRY CHRISTMAS!

WEDNESDAY, DECEMBER 28

Well...Bob fell during therapy again. He just got up from his chair to take a walk and he caught his right toe. Unfortunately, it was a therapist that hasn't worked with Bob much and didn't realize he just needs a little pull to keep him up. He kind of gently landed on a cushy stool, banged his knee and scraped his right forearm. No worries. All is well. He was more worried about the therapist. She's 9 weeks pregnant and very emotional so they both had a good cry together. I handed out the Kleenex and told them it really wasn't anything to shed tears over. His first month at Allegan has been awesome and today was beyond words. After his little meeting with the floor, he sprang back up and walked more than 200 feet without his cane. Speech therapy was brilliant! He's moved up 3 levels since we started at Allegan. He really wants to drive again and it's keeping him motivated. I think 6 days away from therapy made a HUGE difference too. We'll have to remember to take a mini-vacation every few weeks. It's great for Bob and for me! We're having a great holiday season and wish the best for everyone in the new year! GO BOB!

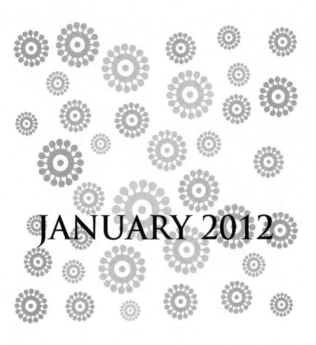

JANUARY 2012

WEDNESDAY, JANUARY 4

We have tons of snow here in Michigan and our lake is almost frozen. It's pretty but a challenge to navigate. We ventured out yesterday to get milk at the local party store and it was the first time out of the house since Sunday morning. Bob's doing fantastically well. I think the break from therapy was just what he needed. We're back at it today with therapy this afternoon. Thank goodness the snow has stopped...hopefully for the week. Looks like more snow this weekend so we'll be playing games and doing exercises inside. GO BOB!

SATURDAY, JANUARY 7

Bob continues his incredible progress. This week the speech therapist told him that he's keeping her really busy trying to keep up with his progress. She had exercises planned for Friday but after his incredible session on Wednesday, she had to redo everything and make things more challenging. It's fantastic to see how far he's come and continues to go. Even after three therapy sessions back to back, he was in good spirits and joking with everyone. During his last session yesterday, the therapist told him he was a "spitfire." HA!

His energy level is amazing. Part of that is due to finally resolving some of his sleep issues. For the last few nights, he's slept a good 6 or 7 hours straight thru. Usually he sleeps for about 3 hrs and then wakes up and continues to do that for about 12 hours. Now he's starting to have a more normal sleep pattern...YAY!

Sunny and warmer here today so we'll be outside as much as possible before the snow comes again. The man loves being outside so we'll bundle up and away we go. GO BOB!

SUNDAY, JANUARY 8

11 months ago today our lives took a completely different direction. Bob's injury changed everything. Our new journey has been quite remarkable and completely unpredictable. Every day brings new challenges and new successes. We had a wonderful weekend with friends playing cards, laughing (a lot!) and just enjoying each other's company. Bob is an incredible human being. His attitude, determination and ability to face every new challenge head on is remarkable. He is so strong, both physically and mentally. I can't begin to imagine what it's like to have pain all the time and then be told to "keep stretching and working those muscles." He's a super man for sure. God has blessed us and we are truly thankful. GO BOB!

SUNDAY, JANUARY 15

Happy Birthday Ang!

Bob continues his phenomenal progress. His memory is improving by the day. We went out for lunch yesterday and this morning he told me he had a good time with Ang and the grandkids and that his French toast was really good. These kinds of things always bring tears to my eyes :) The brain is a powerful thing. Exercises at home are going really well, too. Every day after breakfast we have about an hour of stretching and exercises. His right arm is doing great. He can extend it from his shoulder out so he can shake hands. He extends his hand to everyone he sees so he can keep that arm working. His participation in his own therapy is super! This morning he told me he hopes to play golf again. We have about a foot of snow right now so we'll keep working on the golf swing INSIDE for now. We have to shovel more snow today so we'll bundle up and try to stay warm. It's about 15 degrees right now but at least it's not windy...yet. GO BOB!

WEDNESDAY, JANUARY 18

Bob had his first real beer this weekend...yay! The doc approved one beer a week so he finally had a Bud Light. I asked him if it was everything he ever wanted in a beer and he said, "Eh...it's OK." He drank about half while we played cards with friends and then ditched the rest. He slept like a rock that night so maybe we're onto something. He continues to make great progress during therapy. It's amazing to see his right arm working more and more. The key is for him to use it during normal daily activities and he IS!!!!! More YAY! Another snow storm coming in tonight so we'll be out shoveling again tomorrow. Bob loves to be outside helping with as much as he can. I love his enthusiasm and his ability to get up and go every day is a testament to his strength and attitude. GO BOB!

One more thing...Bob's sense of humor is side splitting! My brother was doing something ridiculous one day and Bob said to him, and I quote, "Are you out of your ever lovin' mind?"

I laughed so hard it made Bob laugh and then we were all laughing. We do a lot of laughing here in our household!!!

THURSDAY, JANUARY 19

Bob went to the eye doc today and we found out he has a depth perception issue and his eyes are not working together. Easily corrected with prisms in his reading glasses. He won't have to wear glasses all the time but it will help with his up-close vision. The ophthalmologist specializes in brain injury survivors and she was awesome. She gave Bob a little pep talk at the end of the visit and told him that it could take up to 8 years to see the full effect of his improvements. She told him to keep going and keep up the good work. She also told him that from a vision standpoint, he will have no issues with driving. My prayers are for Bob to safely do the things he wants to do...whatever those might be. Another great day for Bob. GO BOB!

TUESDAY, JANUARY 24

Bob's new recliner should be here by the end of the week... but working with insurance companies and equipment providers is like trying to shovel Michigan snow with a spoon. It eventually will get done but who can really guess how long it will take. His new recliner will allow him to get up and out of his chair on his own. I know it will make him feel better about his abilities and it will definitely make him more independent. GO BOB!

FRIDAY, JANUARY 27

Bob's new chair came yesterday...YAY! He can get up and go whenever he wants. It's beautiful! He just needs someone near by to make sure he's steady on his feet. Amazing how small his other recliner looks next to his new chair that actually fits him! Furniture is not made for people who are 6'4" that's for sure! Therapy was rough today and his arm is very painful. Now he's resting and watching the Farmer's Insurance Open at Torrey Pines on the golf channel...from his new chair. Jack's making dinner and I'm playing on the computer. Life is good. GO BOB!

MONDAY, JANUARY 30

Bob had a great day in therapy today. He stunned his physical therapist and it made me laugh. He said he couldn't wait for good weather so he could ride his bike so she said, "How about we try the stationary bike today?" So she called over another PT to help get Bob on the bike. She was afraid he wouldn't be able to lift his leg over because it doesn't have a seat that will turn to let him sit down. So they get to the bike, Bob stands up, lifts his left leg over the bike (which means all of his weight was on his right leg) and climbs on the bike. He sits down, she looks at him with this face like "Holy crap" and then he says, "Well, you told me to get on the bike." Ha! :) He's getting so STRONG! Another great thing - he stood at the sink and rinsed the dishes after supper. That's such a normal thing for him to do it was wonderful. I love how independent he's getting and how he's really pushing himself throughout the day. He still has pain in his right arm all the time but he pushes through it and keeps going. He's my miracle man!!!! GO BOB!

FEBRUARY 2012

SATURDAY, FEBRUARY 4

Bob finally has his new glasses and he's getting a new less-bulky foot brace...YAY! His right foot is getting so strong he only needs to wear the brace when walking so they're going to give him a spring-action brace that's more flexible and easier to walk in. I'm so happy for him! He's walking more and more around the house and I'm hoping this new brace will make it even easier. It's been such a mild winter he's already talking about walking out to the boat to go fishin'. He also keeps telling me "we" need to clean the garage. Since that's always been his domain, I'm surprised he's going to let me help. He has his own man-room off the garage with all his "stuff" in it. Once spring gets here, we'll be spending some time getting that thing all neat and tidy, too. I'll have to ask for special permission to go into the man-room but I'm sure he'll let me at least for a little while. He continues to make great progress during therapy and now they're going to have him do more and more work on the stationary bike to build up his endurance. He told me yesterday to never take walking for granted because you never know when it's going to be hard...and yes I had a tear in my eye for him. He's working so incredibly hard to get back as much function and independence as he can!!! He continues to amaze me every day. I marvel at his work ethic and his ability to keep on pushing himself. We are so incredibly fortunate!!!! GO BOB!

WEDNESDAY, FEBRUARY 8

For the rest of my life, I will forever know exactly what I was doing on February 8 at 7:00 pm - a memory no one should ever have to keep (and thank goodness a memory Bob will never regain). However, given the catastrophic nature of Bob's injury and the unknown outcome (which is still unknown), we are incredibly blessed and fortunate. Diffuse Axonal Injury is what Bob sustained one year ago today. If you have a chance, google it sometime and see what the internet has to say about the prognosis. It's very scary but Bob has defied the odds!!! I'm in awe of the progress Bob has made in just one year. His drive, determination, work ethic, desire for perfection, strength, sense of humor and ability to just keep doing the things he needs to do are a testament to what makes Bob Bob. We've cried together, laughed together, disagreed with each other, teased each other but more than anything else we HAVE each other and that is what is so amazing to me. He is a very special guy and I'm learning great and wonderful things both FROM him and ABOUT him every day. He continues his journey to become the best BOB he can be, which is what we all should strive to do regardless of our limitations. We continue to find strength from our incredible family, friends, neighbors and co-workers. Thank you for all that you continue to do for us. GO BOB!

SUNDAY, FEBRUARY 19

We're having a great weekend. Bob leaves his chair at home now when we run errands. He walks out to the car and then back in, mostly without his cane. He just carries it for security. Next week in therapy he'll be trying just a single normal looking cane. Right now he uses a cane with four feet on the bottom. He's pretty excited about moving to just a normal cane. He also gets his new brace on Wednesday. It's smaller and lighter and he'll be able to get it on and off by himself. He continues to do more and more for himself and doesn't like it when people do too much. One of the attendants was trying to put his shoes on for him and he told her, "I can do that. Just give me my shoes." Of course, she was trying to put them on the wrong feet...duh :) I love that he wants to do stuff by himself. He is also able to zip up his own jacket...VERY COOL! Most of the time I have to sit on my hands or pretend to be busy doing something else so I don't jump in too early to help. Bob's really good about asking for help BEFORE he gets too frustrated. He always wants to at least try something first. IT'S A BEAUTIFUL THING! GO BOB!

WEDNESDAY, FEBRUARY 22

Bob has his new brace today. It is smaller, lighter and he can put it on by himself. He was so happy he gave the orthotics guy a hug and then had tears in his eyes. Then in therapy he got to try a new regular cane. He was so happy about that he had tears in his eyes again. Of course I cried because he was so happy. I love happy tears but it's hard to tell if I'm happy or sad. I definitely have an ugly cry. Today was a beautiful day. GO BOB!

SATURDAY, FEBRUARY 25

We're snowed in again here in Allegan, Michigan. It's crazy how much snow this little area gets. Of course, the radar shows the biggest bluest band of snow right over our little town. It's beautiful but this house is too small to stay inside one more day. We're going to venture outside today even if it's just on the front porch. We need some fresh air! Bob's doing more wonderful things. Yesterday we had to skip therapy because we had too much snow so we did a bunch of stuff at home. The speech therapist gave us a bunch of worksheets so we worked on handwriting and multi-step directions. He tried similar versions of some of the worksheets about 3 months ago at MFB and they were way too difficult and frustrating. I was a little nervous for him when we got them out yesterday but he aced them! In fact, two of them were too easy! AMAZING! GO BOB!

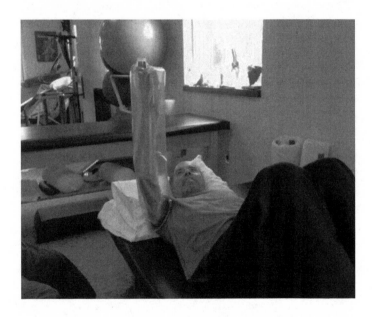

APRIL 2012

SUNDAY, APRIL 1

Wow...it's been awhile since we wrote anything to let you guys know what's going on. So much has happened for the good. Bob is walking all over the house now. He's getting stronger and stronger and wants to get rid of the wheel chair. With the good weather, we've been able to walk outside so we go downtown Allegan and walk on the boardwalk. It's the perfect place to practice and Bob loves it. The rest of the home renovations should be starting soon. Bob will be able to get out to the boat to go fishing. It sure will be nice when that's ready and the good weather is here to stay. Looking forward to a great summer. We're on vacation this week. No work for me and no therapy for Bob. We have a ton of stuff planned and we're just going to have some fun. Wednesday we're going to lunch with the kids and then to the butter-fly exhibit at Meijer gardens. When the sun is out this week, we'll be walking on the boardwalk and if it's warm enough, we'll have lunch in the park. We also have coffee in the mornings on the deck as long as it's not freezing! Bob continues his incredible progress keeping his amazing attitude and doing everything they tell him to do. GO BOB!

MAY 2012

SUNDAY, MAY 20

Did ya ever have one of those days? Yesterday was that day for us. We finally have air conditioning in our house and we were so excited to use it. Yesterday it was 87 out and today it's 90! So we turned on our air, it ran for 3 hours and the house went from 75 to 80 degrees! What? That's not right. Then we were out for our evening stroll and Bob's wheelchair cushion popped. So we came back inside, he sat in his lift chair and the lift mechanism made this horrible squeaky noise and then bumped him back in his chair. CRAZY! So we opened the windows, turned on the fan, went to bed and threw the covers over our heads! The good news - air conditioning guy came back today and fixed the air, we had an extra cushion for the wheelchair so we're using that today and the lift chair seems to be working OK...at least until we can have someone come look at it next week. Bob continues his incredible progress in spite of the crazy weird things happening to his stuff! He's experiencing more pain on his right side because the therapists are having him do more so we're trying to find the right balance. He's an amazing guy and I continue to learn so much from him. GO BOB!

On the golf course, 2013...GO BOB!

CONCLUSION

This journal documents Bob's journey navigating life after a brain injury. It is just the first 16 months of what will be a life time of adjusting, relearning and adapting. Bob spent nearly 3 years in out-patient therapy at Mary Free Bed completing formal therapy in June of 2014. He continues with a daily exercise program both at home and through his membership at the YMCA. Bob continues to be a positive, uplifting and happy man. It is truly a blessing and a joy to have him with us. We continue to be thankful and feel very blessed with the support from family, friends, coworkers and people we haven't even met. We would love to hear from you. Please email us at bckamps1@gmail.com and share your story or let us know your thoughts on this journal.

RECAP OF BOB'S STAY IN INSTITUTIONS:

- 5 weeks in critical care at Borgess Medical Center – Kalamazoo, MI

- 2 weeks in long term acute care at Borgess Pip Hospital – Plainwell, MI

- 3 months in skilled nursing/rehabilitation at Spectrum Neuro-Rehab – Grand Rapids, MI

- 2 months in acute rehabilitation at Mary Free Bed hospital – Grand Rapids, MI

- 3 years in out-patient rehabilitation at Mary Free Bed hospital – Grand Rapids, MI

OUR BASIC FOUNDATION IN DEALING WITH A BRAIN INJURY:

• Every injury is different and everyone heals differently.

• Be patient and rejoice in every positive accomplishment no matter how small YOU might think it is.

• Accept the person for who they are after the brain injury; they will be different but different isn't necessarily a bad thing.

• No matter how hard an event or situation is for you, imagine how difficult it is for the person with the brain injury.

• Be open to trying the things you used to do just in a different way. Bob is able to use an adaptive golf cart to hit golf balls at the driving range. This is our way of golfing now.

• Approach everything from a positive point of view. Rather than saying, "don't forget to brush your teeth," try saying, "remember to brush your teeth."